# Beckenham
# The Home Front 1939-45

### Cliff Watkins & Pat Manning

*'Beckenham is not far from my home in the heart of beautiful Kent. It stands in the well known track of 'Bomb Alley' and I fear that many marks of those ordeals still remain among you.'*

Winston Churchill receiving the Freedom of Beckenham
October 1946

First published in Great Britain 2005
Second edition reprinted with amendments November 2005

Copyright © 2005 Cliff Watkins and Pat Manning


ISBN 0-9540202-2-7


Published by

# Jenna Publishing

59 Staddiscombe Road, Plymouth, PL9 9NA

on behalf of of the Bromley Borough Local History Society,
Registered Charity No.273963

Front Cover photographs: Corner of Church and St. George's Roads (July 1944) and the Christ Church Area (January 1945) scenes of two of the worst V1 attacks in Beckenham.

Frontispiece photograph: Firemen from Beckenham Fire station have a break from filling sand bags 1939 in Bromley Road. (MC)

Designed by Chris Edwards, Lancasters  www.lancasters.co.uk
Printed and bound by CPI Group (UK) Ltd, Croydon, CR0 4YY

# Contents

# List of Appendices

# Foreword

The Home Front is a record of some of the memories and experiences of the people of Beckenham and Penge during the Second World War. Its brief life-sketches throw a clear and brilliant light on the lives of people whose courage and perseverance had little public acknowledgement or applause. Much of what they tell is incredibly moving. Some of the stories have been written down by the people concerned and some are the result of interviews conducted by The Home Front authors.

The book was put together by Pat Manning and Cliff Watkins in an impressively short space of time, in order to coincide with VE/VJ Day sixty year celebrations. The Appendices at the back will be an invaluable resource for other historians wishing to do research, and the authors are to be saluted for the immense amount of hard work that went into the project. The focus on the Beckenham and Penge side of our Borough is particularly welcome. Home Front left me wanting to know more, my mind buzzing with questions; I hope very much that a further collection will be possible.

Veronica Lloyd, 2005

AFS firemen in procession through Penge High Street with a replica of the London Fireboat, Massey Shaw, during Penge Weapons Week, April 19 to 26, 1941.

At the end of May 1940, the Massey Shaw joined the tugs towing strings of small boats, yachts, lifeboats and even dinghies down the Thames to help with the evacuation from Dunkirk. She ferried some 600 soldiers to safety and later that year she was in action again fighting the blitz on the London Docks with help from Beckenham firemen.

# Contributors and Dramatis Personae

| | | |
|---|---|---|
| EA | Edna | Antrobus |
| EB | Ellen | Barbet |
| CB | Carey | Blyton |
| JB1 | John | Blundell |
| JB2 | Jean | Bogle (aka Hazel Cummings) |
| MB | Mollie | Bowles |
| FB | Felicity | Boyden (nee Edden) |
| AB | Alfred | Breck |
| TB | Tony | Bristow |
| RB | Ray | Burden |
| JC | June | Carmichael (nee Farmer) |
| RC | Dr Ron | Cox |
| GC | Geoffrey | Crabb |
| MC | Mavis | Crawford (nee Leeks) |
| GC | Gerald | Crease |
| WD | William | Duckworth |
| MD | Monica | Duncan (nee Weeks) |
| DF | Dot | Figg |
| YF | Yvonne | Fish (aka Sue Fish) |
| PF | Peter | Forster |
| PG | Peter | Grey |
| OH | Olive | Hamer (formerly Mountjoy, nee Beadle) |
| JH | Jack | Hilton |
| AH 1 | Arthur | Holden |
| AH 2 | Allen | Horsley |
| TJ | Tony | Johns (Antony Copeland Johns) |
| DJ | David | Johnson |
| JJ | Jill | Jones |
| PJ | Peter | Jones |
| JK | Jill | Kite (nee Maynard) |
| JL | Janet | Lambert |
| ML | Margaret | Lambert |
| SM | Stephanie | Maltman |
| PM | Pat | Manning (nee Ridler) |
| MM | Mary | McInally |
| HO | Helen | Oliver (nee Lyford) |
| MO | Martin | Ormes |
| CP | Chris | Porteous |
| MP | Mave | Preedy (nee Covey) |
| CP | Christine | Purnell |
| PR | Peter | Rees |
| JR | Joan | Rees (nee Burns) |
| OR | Olive | Rippengal |
| MR | Mollie | Russell-Smith (aka Mrs Lunggren, Mrs Frost) |
| MS | Mrs | S. |
| VS | Valerie | Sheldon (nee Thornton) |
| ES | Eric | Smith |
| DS | Douglas | Smith |
| HS | Howard | Smith |
| FS | Frank | Somerville |
| JS | Joyce | Stanley (nee Stonham) |
| VS | Veronica | Surman |
| HT | Harold | Tatman |
| ET | E. J. | Thomason |
| BT | Bernard | Tyson |
| NW | Neil | Walters |
| CW | Cliff | Watkins |
| VW | Veronica | Watkins (nee Jones) |
| FW | Francis | Weiss |
| FWJ | Francis | Weiss Junior |
| BW | Brenda | Wheatley (nee Banks) |
| JW | John | Williams |
| PW 2 | Pat | Williams |
| VW | Vanessa | Williamson |
| PW | Peter | Wiseman |
| DW | David | Wood |

Beckenham crew at work on London wharves in December 1940.
Painting by Beckenham AFS member, J Kingsley Sutton (RB)

# One
# Beckenham Gets Ready

'The gutters of London will run with blood,' said Great Aunt Rose in September 1938. She was reading the tea leaves concerning the coming war. My parents realised how this echoed the newspapers of the time but my father did not want such thoughts in the middle of our idyllic deepest Devon holiday at Capton Farm. He dismissed Aunt Rose as an eccentric rustic. A year later my father was asking Aunt Rose for help with the evacuation of his wife and three children.

David Johnson

Opening of new Fire Station in Glebe Way, West Wickham, in 1939 (MC)

Nineteen thirty five was a proud year for the new borough of Beckenham. Joined with West Wickham the year before, the two towns were ready to show that they were worthy of running their own affairs. Although Penge remained a separate UDC, services like schools, fire service and ambulance were shared with its wealthier neighbour and most of us regarded Penge as part of Beckenham. Among the buildings planned for the next few years were a fire station in Glebe Way, a branch library in West Wickham, a central post office by the Beckenham war memorial, a central Beckenham library by the swimming baths, an extension to the Cottage Hospital, a joint maternity hospital for Beckenham & Penge in Stonepark Ave and an Odeon cinema at Elmers End Green. However as early as 1935, the Home Office was forming its first ARP department and the shadow of war was threatening to cloud the forthcoming celebrations for the Coronation of George VI.

A meeting in 1937 in the Grand Hall of the Beckenham Baths attracted well over a thousand people whose prime worry was of the possibility of a gas attack. Questions covered whether children would be provided with gas masks, what would we do with our pets and how could we protect ourselves against mustard gas.

Cllr Sampson, Chairman of the Air Raid Precautions Committee, asked for some 1,500 volunteers at the 1937 meeting. They were in seven groups, VAD (Voluntary Aid Detachment) and Red Cross, Wardens, Heavy and Light Rescue, Ambulance and Transport, Despatch riders, Telephonists and additional firefighters as the AFS.

Beckenham Post Office, built 1939 (CW)

Beckenham Civil Defence Committee 1939-45
seated outside the main entrance to the Town Hall (FB)

These services were eventually known as the Civil Defence and included the Metropolitan and Special Police, Auxiliary Ambulance Drivers, the WVS (Women's Voluntary Service) and even ENSA (Entertainments National Service Association). The service expected from an ambulance driver cannot be better described than that given by Violet Cruikshank (Cruiky) who had already lost her father, brother and fiancé in the 1914 war in France. Violet volunteered at the outbreak of war when there was no proper equipment, furniture, ambulances, sleeping quarters or mess room but Cruiky turned everything into a delicious adventure. It was on the night of 9 September 1940 when the group on duty had Cruiky keeping up their spirits and she went out in one of the first two ambulances to leave. The four women never returned. The two ambulances had been hit by a HE bomb as they waited outside a blazing building to load casualties.

The Chief Officer of the Beckenham Fire Service, J H P Evans, died within a few days of his retirement in June 1937 but he had brought Beckenham's fire appliances up to the high standard that would be needed during the blitz of 1940/41. Although Beckenham's fire service was as up to date as any in the country, the bombing revealed the shortcomings of many outlying districts as appliances were incompatible. Chief Officer Netherwood from Beckenham was appointed a Fire Force Commander and transferred to Leicestershire to impart his expertise.

However it was such discrepancies among the various London councils that led to today's London Boroughs already being planned before the end of the war.

A trial blackout was held from 12.30 to 4.00 am on the night of 9/10 August but most residents avoided it by going to bed! The street lights went out at 11.30 pm and cars used only their side lights. The occasional illuminated window disclosed a brilliant light by contrast to the black darkness but the blackout was mostly perfect. Wardens, special constables and AFS took advantage of the enforced blackout to have half hourly 'raids' causing 'fires' in Cherry Tree Walk, Lloyds Way and Croydon Rd, Elmers End, assuming bombs had knocked out telephones.

This was followed by a second 'wave' in Goddard Rd, Bramerton Rd and Wellhouse Rd and finally a third at Eden Rd, Crossways and Merlin Grove. How much sleep did the Eden Park residents have that night? The following account comes from Francis Weiss who in 1938, shortly after Munich, was turned down twice by the Officers' Emergency Reserve (OER) because he was not British although he spoke five languages and had 4½ years WW1 experience and special training with the Tyrolean Rifles. He was told to volunteer for some other form of national service so he reported to the ARP. It was now August 1939 and he wrote:

*'I visit my family who are on holiday. We pack for the return home to Beckenham, take a last stroll along the still peaceful beaches. People go about as usual; there are some worried faces, but others seem to take no notice of events. My younger son, now nine years old, holds my hand. "Are you feeling cold Daddy?" "No, I am not cold"; but my hands are icy and my heart frozen ... War! The horrors I know so well and now my family will be in it!*

*"Daddy, I would like to see the Bird Museum once more." We go in; he inspects glass case after case, carefully noting every detail: stuffed birds, eggs and nests. How he loves it! My feet feel like clay; there is a cold steel ring round my skull, and my eyes are burning. War! ...There he stands, this little, fair boy of mine, interested and smiling. Can he realise what this means? War ...And the other boy who is sixteen, and their mother, and all the other millions of mother and children? To know that one is to some minute extent responsible for all this! War. The word repeats itself, like a mocking, sickening, cuckoo-clock. War. War. War.*

*We are home again. There are feverish preparations; sandbags are piled up, cases full of rubble and earth. In our home? Can it be possible? Windows have to be secured against blast, twenty years after a lunacy that killed off over twelve millions of innocent people! Are they all mad? What is all this? Have I to ask myself if our home is safe for my family? Am I dreaming? I inspect the shelter. Suddenly, like clear water welling up through a cracked white surface of ice, there comes to me the memory of our dug outs in WW1... Where are our gas-masks?*

*September 3rd. Barrage balloons go up swaying in the air: strange clumsy silver sausages. Big Ben has a hollow sound and Mr Chamberlain's voice is tired and sad.*

The diary 'Milestones' of Edward (Ted) James Burns of 65 Glanfield Rd provides an insight into the effect of the war on an ordinary family. Ted was a tea broker for S S Smith in the City. He writes:

*'In the summer of 1939, life was very sweet, playing tennis, bowls and golf and taking hikes in the country but on 3 September 1939, Mr Chamberlain declared war on Germany. The tea trade was in a hopeless mess and I nearly joined up as a full time fireman. I had enlisted part time in the AFS in 1938. We had to put up curtains to stop the light showing which was very depressing. Joan's school (Marian Vian) closed and the London children were evacuated. There were air raid shelters everywhere and buildings were sandbagged. Christmas was very quiet, rationing has been mentioned and our life is being put out of gear'.*

Ted with daughter Joan. (JR)

# Two
# The Phoney War ends as the Battle of Britain begins

On what must have been the morning of Tuesday 4 June 1940, a long line of London & North Eastern railway coaches was held up at the signal gantry at the bottom of the Beckenham & Penge Grammar School for Boys school field. Boys' started going to the tuck shop for cakes and biscuits and taking them with jugs of water up the embankment to the bedraggled, dirty French and Belgian soldiers that packed the trains.

Dr Ron Cox

At the newly opened Odeon at Elmers End, the first day of the war, 3rd September 1939, saw Ray Milland star in 'Easy Living.' Much to our surpise life seemed to be going as usual.

Until the spring of 1940 very little of military importance happened in Western Europe and the expected Blitzkrieg on London and other major cities was a non event. Beckenham families returned from their private evacuation and it seemed as though nothing was happening. This was the period of the 'Phoney War'

However things were happening without the public's awareness. The liner Athenia was attacked and sunk by a U-boat killing 112 of the 1,102 passengers and crew on the day war broke out. Millions of propaganda leaflets were dropped over Germany so that the Germans would read about the evils of Nazi Germany and realise that they were vulnerable to attack. The British Expeditionary Force (BEF) had joined the French forces to contain the spread of the German Army to the West. Captain Philip Vian (nephew of Marian Vian) rescued British merchant seamen from the Altmark in a fjord in Norway in February 1940.

Blackout was rigidly enforced from 1 September 1939 until it became obvious that it was resulting in many deaths on the roads. The first Beckenham fatalities of the blackout occurred on the first day of the war. A lorry ran into a slight collision between two cars by the Crown Inn, Bromley Common. Unbelievably a fire started because someone lit a match. This resulted in the death of Sheila Huffner from Mays Hill Rd and John Rollo Elstob from Manor Rd. A few days later, another woman, Mabel Heasman, was knocked down by a bus in Parish Lane and died from multiple injuries in Beckenham hospital.

The blackout brought about a 40% increase in road deaths and a jingle was published to try to make people aware of the danger.

> 'When walking after dark at night
> For safety's sake wear something white'

On 22 January 1940, 'WWII car headlamps' (i.e. existing lamps covered by paper tape) were introduced and a 20mph speed limit was imposed in built up areas.

In January 1940 Ted Burns was very depressed and he wrote in his diary

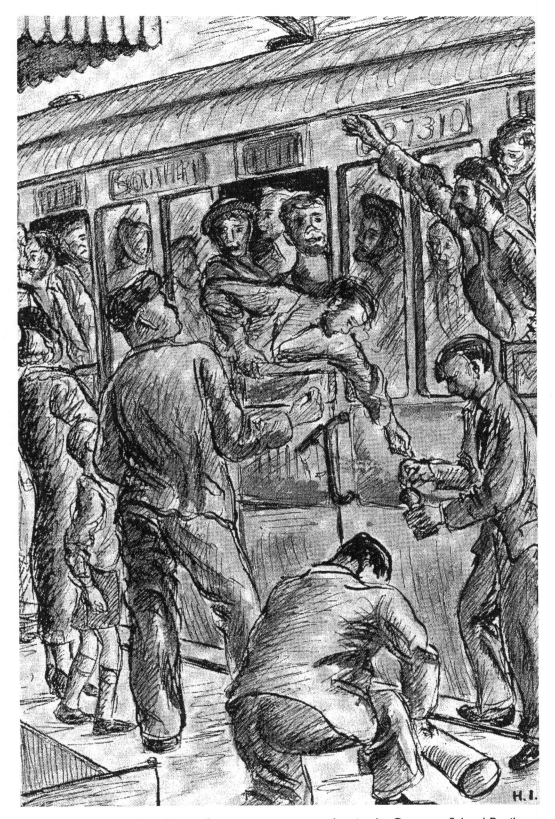

Dunkirk Evacuees at Kent House Station contemporary drawing by Grammar School Pupil (AHI)

*'This is a really bad month. The weather is the worst for a century. It has been very cold with fog, rain and heavy snow. Butter, bacon and sugar are rationed, coal is short, travelling awful and all you can do in the evening is listen to the wireless.'*

By April 1940, the Wehrmacht had pushed the French and British armies back with lightning speed to the coast and on May 26 1940, 'Operation Dynamo' began to evacuate the troops from Dunkirk.

The seas remained absolutely calm. The RAF, much maligned by the Army at the time, fought vehemently to deny the enemy total air supremacy over the beaches. By 4 June, 350,000 of the professional soldiers of the British Expeditionary Force and some 120,000 French troops were saved from the beaches of Dunkirk, helped by the fact that Hitler never ordered a full scale attack on them by his Panzer tank crews and dive bombers.

The following account of the returning soldiers in the trains greeted by the Grammar School boys appeared in the Beckenham Journal 8 June 1940 and was printed in the school magazine, the Beccehamian.

> *'The boys dived their hands into their pockets from which came an assortment of sweets, chocolates and biscuits, offered generously, if a little shyly, to these wild looking men. All along the train boys were chatting away in French with the soldiers. Soon souvenirs were being exchanged and everyone was happy, the French because of their warm welcome, which they had not expected from the phlegmatic English and the boys because of the friendliness of the soldiers. Among the soldiers one would have found English cigarettes, postcards, pencils and school caps. The boys had French money, buttons, penknives and even a ring. As each train left, the boys shouted words of encouragement, "Au revoir" and "Bonne chance" and a Frenchman scribbled on a card "Cet acceuil si chalereux, nous n'oublierons jamais" (Never shall we forget such a warm welcome).'*

Spitfire Advert. The money raised bought a plane, named Beckenham, one of the invicta Squadron.

Tony Johns saw the bandaged injured soldiers on the trains between Dover and Victoria throwing out letters at Beckenham Junction station hoping the locals would post messages to their relatives to show they were rescued from Dunkirk.

It is possible that Hitler was hoping that Britain would come to peace terms with him and there were members of the government who would have done so. However, Winston Churchill had taken over from Neville Chamberlain on 10 May 1940 and he gained the loyalty and confidence of the British people. With Churchill as the Leader of a coalition government, we never had any doubt that we would win the war. He was such an accomplished orator that he convinced us all even in the darkest moments that victory would be ours as he proceeded to mastermind the Battle of Britain, the North African Campaign and to persuade the USA to come to our aid.

Churchill's speech on the 4 June 1940 ended with

> *'We shall fight on the beaches. We shall fight on the landing grounds. We shall fight in the fields, and in the streets. We shall fight in the hills. We shall never surrender.'*

The phoney war was well and truly at an end.

Churchill spoke again on the 18 June as follows.

> *'The battle of France is over, **I expect the Battle of Britain is about to begin**. Upon this battle depends the survival of Christian civilisation. Upon it depends our own British life. The whole fury and might of the enemy must very soon be turned on us. Hitler knows that he will have to break us in this island or lose the war.*

*If we can stand up to him, all Europe may be free but if we fail then the whole world will sink into the Abyss of a new Dark Age. Let us therefore brace ourselves to our duties and so bear ourselves that, if the British Empire and its Commonwealth last for a thousand years, men will still say "This was their finest hour."'*

There followed desperate air battles. The crisis was reached on 15 August when all the resources of Fighter Command in the South were being used. Between 24 August and 6 September 1940 the German attack was directed against the RAF airfields in the South, including of course, our Biggin Hill. It was during visits to the airfields that Churchill coined the phrase that he used in his stirring speech on 20 August to the House of Commons, *'Never in the field of human conflict was so much owed by so many to so few.'*

One of the most patriotic ideas was to start a 'Spitfire Fund' to raise £5,000 for a Spitfire. The meeting on Thursday night 29 August 1940 at the Public Hall was followed a few hours later by bombs demolishing two houses with three fatal casualties.

From 6 September the Luftwaffe changed to night bombing having failed to win the Battle of Britain against the RAF and the London Blitz had begun.

The Luftwaffe mounted a powerful attack on the London docks. On 7 September we were mesmerised as the sky became full of rows of German bombers heading towards the London docks. Almost 1000 German planes were involved, 348 bombers and 617 fighter escorts. We were beneath the dogfights as the RAF engaged the German fighter planes. Enormous fires were started in the docks that continued into the night and the next day lighting the target for the night raids that lasted until the 10th May, 1941.

The school summer holidays were ending in an almost unceasing succession of Warnings and All Clear signals coming to a climax on 15 September, 1940 when we in Beckenham watched the battle going on overhead in a cloudless sky. Jack Hilton and his cousin watched the sky over Biggin Hill.

*'It was a hive of activity, white vapour trails filling the sky with individual "dog-fights" everywhere. To our child like minds every one shot down was German.'*

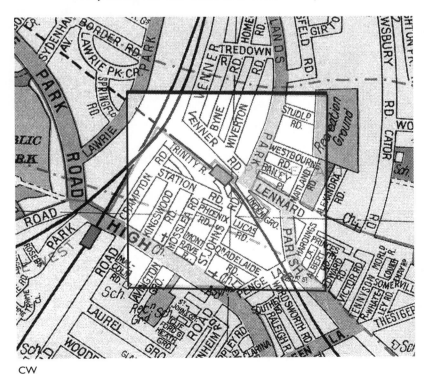

CW

About midday on that Sunday, a formation of eighteen raiders appeared that dropped 72 small bombs in an area one-quarter of a mile square round Penge East station, some still unexploded by the next morning. Jack Hilton recalls the afternoon when bombs were dropped at the bottom of the road, adjacent to the main London - Kent railway. He has learnt that it was a deliberate raid to take out Penge tunnel, Herne Hill Station and Battersea railway bridge. Miraculously, there were no casualties in Penge from that attack but we had moved into the front line!

Marjorie Sear was bombed out from 22 St. John's Rd by bombs that fell at the junction of Lucas and St. John's Rd.

# Three
# The Blitz

'I think we were all aware of the danger the firemen faced. The bombs fell virtually every night and the men were constantly on duty tackling fires, saving people. Beckenham was directly on the flight path to London and the planes used to fly over all the time'

**Mollie Bowles fireman's widow**

The first bomb to fall on Beckenham landed on 26 August 1940 in the field of the Yokohama Specie Bank Athletic Club in Worsley Bridge Rd, now the Footsie Club. Leaving a large crater in a field notorious for

flooding since it was the flood plain of the River Pool, wags from the factories shouted 'That'll improve the drainage!' This had been preceded by two small bombs from a lone night raider earlier in the month that had fallen just across the borough boundary in Lewisham but had shattered the windows of the John Bell, Hills and Lucas factory by Lower Sydenham station.

Friday of the same week saw the first deaths from the bombing as a bomb on 78 Clockhouse Rd killed Nellie and Walter Glenny and Mabel Vincent. As the blitz started there were non-stop air raids for 47 days beginning on 7 September.

Yokohama Specie Bank Athletic Club in Worsley Bridge Rd (PM)

There had been raids elsewhere in Kent as described by Dr Ron Cox who had been taking his School Certificate exams with the instruction that if you hear anything falling, get under the desks but don't talk! Returning from a cycle ride through Pratt's Bottom, he and Ray Greenwood witnessed from a distance of nine miles or so the raid on 15 August at Croydon Airport where 62 people were killed and many injured when twenty two HEs were dropped.

Surrey Docks (SM)

The raids continued until 10 May 1941 with the longest over the weekend of 14 to 17 September 1940 and the most severe on the night of 16/17 April 1941 when 40 were killed and 133 injured and all Beckenham's resources were used at once. The names of the casualties and the roads where bombs, HE, parachute mines and incendiaries fell as far as we have been able to ascertain are given in the appendix.

Rear view of 21-25 Broomfield Rd after bombing, October 1940 (CW)

E J Thomason joined Muirhead's in June 1940 aged 17 as an Instrument Maker Improver. He saw the aeroplanes milling about in the sky when he looked through the windows towards Croydon. He understood at the time that they were Italian planes bombing Croydon Airport. Our fighters attacked them and we were told that none of the Italian planes returned to base. Later when he was in the RAF, he heard that a German fighter flew over Muirheads spraying bullets from tree height, wounding the milkman's horse and narrowly missing one of the Muirhead employees.

David Johnson writes of the time when his family were bombed out.

*'At 2 am on 20 September 1940 we were saved injury or death by our shelter. The Mission Hall in Parish Lane had been wrecked. No more Wolf Cub meetings or services there. People we knew had been killed. Our severely blasted house was uninhabitable. My kind genteel Alexandra Junior School teacher, Miss Percy, had visited us during her lunch time. She was relieved we were only dirty and hungry. "Go to the shelters at the Grammar school."*

*We went there that night. I was impressed by the care of the older schoolboys perhaps 14 years old who seemed to run the shelter, even the unpleasant latrine duties. After living half the time in the shelter for a few days we arranged to go to Aunt Rose privately. Our mother bought us new caps from the Whitehall Tailors at the corner of Green Lane but I lost mine when I pushed my head out of the train window on the way to Devon from Paddington station.*

*We settled near Newton Abbot and walking back across the fields with my sister from an errand, I was attacked by a gang of village boys. "You are a lot of bullies," I shouted and offered to fight the oldest boy. We had a good fight with even some cheers for me. The boy I was fighting had lost his father at Dunkirk and his family was very poor and undernourished. Their dislike of evacuees was understandable as some of the official ones had been given quality clothing from Canada.'*

9

Another family that spent the blitz in the Grammar school shelters was that of Dot Figg who writes:

*'I was fourteen when the war started and my brother was ten. When the air raids started, we would eat our evening meal straight away, gather up our bedding of a pillow and two blankets and make our way to the Grammar school underground shelters. It was usually crowded and people were very friendly. Some would knit or sew and we young ones would play cards or board games. We used to sing to distract us from the fear of bombs and the noise of gunfire. There were wooden benches for us to sleep on, not very wide and most difficult to turn over on. One lady would turn hers over and sleep on it close to the stone floor which must have felt very cold. Condensation would drip on us and make our bedding damp. I recall a very little girl who would sing the old songs that her grandmother had taught her. My favourite was*

Dot Figg's Odeon Air Raid Shelter (DF)

*Molly Malone. One night we arrived to find the shelter flooded so we went to one by Cottingham Rd instead. With no heating, the shelter was very cold. We spent Christmas at the shelter by the Odeon cinema where we joined up with a family from Barnmead Rd.*

*We decorated the shelter with holly. Our mother made cakes, paste sandwiches and soft drinks with a beer each for the men. We exchanged small gifts like knitted hats and gloves made from old woolly jumpers and took down the wind-up gramophone. We sang and danced and there was no siren that night.*

*Another shelter we tried was in the Penge Recreation ground opposite St John's Church but we didn't go back because the RAF had a barrage balloon in the park. No doubt my mother thought it wasn't safe especially as the balloon took to the air every time a raid was imminent.*

*We were in our own Anderson shelter when we were bombed out and were given a room by the Salvation Army until our house was patched up. Each night we slept in warm bunks in the Warden's Post. My brother, now 14, was allowed to sit in on the wireless messages and watch them plot their charts of aircraft coming across the French coast. What friendships we made in those dangerous times!*

Francis Weiss converted his underground garage into a shelter which was to be their dining room, their bedroom, their home.

*'A faint, faint drone. You feel it almost before the ears can sense it. The drones come nearer and so does the gunfire. Doors and windows rattle; there is a swishing through the air, a whistling followed by shattering thuds. Tragedy somewhere. Flares, search lights, shells; a red glow in the sky; a ghastly firework display. Fragments of shells clatter down on the roofs; bullets crackle like peas thrown against a window. This foul, moist, dugout atmosphere. Now my family has to breathe it.*

*They all sleep. How can they? In this infernal noise! Don't they know what it means, what it can bring? I lie awake for hours, hours. Thuds, explosions somewhere; someone's home is shattered, a life ended. In the morning the children are running about looking for shell splinters as we used to collect minerals. They still play at war. They bomb their tin soldiers with pebbles; a delightful game.'*

Cedars Road (BL)

Dr Ron Cox also recalls those nights spent in the shelters. British Summer Time remained in force during the winter to give people the chance to get home before the raids began.

> *'The problem was what to do with ourselves. Reading was not really possible by the candlelight in our shelter and the tradition arose that I would take my violin and my Uncle Will his harmonica. We would play and sing mainly music hall songs of which my uncle knew a great many. One policeman said that the only thing that kept him going in the rather frail wooden police box at the corner of Grosvenor Rd was the sound of our playing and singing.*
>
> *One time when my father was on leave, from the Navy, an incendiary fell on the very top of our shelter. We quickly climbed out and saw that it had rolled down the covering of soil. We threw buckets of sand over it but had trouble persuading my father not to pour water on it. We had been told that it would cause incendiaries with potassium in them to spit in all directions and perhaps explode.'*

In December 1940 Ted Burns saw his job go floating away down the gutters of docklands. Chests of tea were being washed away by the hoses of the AFS (including Ted) who were fighting the London dock fires. At home, the windows of his house were broken and the ceilings had caved in because a bomb fell behind numbers 36 and 38 Glanfield Rd. Ted employed a builder to bring the Anderson shelter from the garden into the dining room where the family slept for years although his wife and daughter spent some time away in places like Bideford and Lingfield. The reader will be glad to know that after the war he returned to his old job and eventually fulfilled his ambition by being appointed to the Board having started as a tea boy at 13.

On the night of 29 December there was a heavy attack on London and several bombs fell on the north region of Beckenham including two parachute mines that fell silently without the HE's warning whine. Mr Maistre, an air raid warden at the post opposite Holy Trinity church in Lennard Rd, described the incident as follows:

> *'Mr Hargraves and I were standing in a porchway with Mr Nixom watching events. We saw an object which we at first thought was an airman descending by means of a parachute. We watched the object pass over the church and the trees and then continue down the road at the side of the church. We started off in that direction and I was about 15 yards round the corner when there was a blinding flash. I automatically ducked and covered my head but I was picked up and blown across the main road into a garden. A privet hedge broke my fall and the only injury I received was a bruise on my left leg. My colleague had been hit on the head with a brick and needed first aid'.*

The church was seriously damaged, a large number of houses were made uninhabitable and an eleven year old girl, Hazel Burgess, was killed when trapped under the debris of her aunt's preparatory school in the garden of which the bomb had landed. The post duty Warden, Mr Truer, described two explosions and said he had never heard so much noise in his life. Things were falling for at least a minute. Another parachute mine was reported to hit the cable of the barrage balloon in the Ibis sports ground in Cator Road (now Alexandra Junior School) which probably accounted for the second explosion. According to the research of a member of the Air Historical Branch of the Ministry of Defence there were no casualties recorded among the balloon crew.

The death of the Charter Mayor, Sir Josiah Stamp, was among the tragedies that occurred on 'The Wednesday' Beckenham's worst raid when 40 were killed and 133 injured on the night of 16 April 1941. His house, Tantallon at 4 Park Hill Rd, Shortlands was razed to the ground. His wife Baroness Olive Jessie and eldest son the Hon Wilfred Carlyle Stamp died with him with three of the four maids.

**The devastation caused by parachute mine that fell on 93 to 103 Merlin Grove in November 1940.** (BT and AH2)

Elsie Unwin was the only survivor in the cellars of the house which received a direct hit from one of three 500lb bombs to fall. The three maids who died in the cellars were 16 year old Betty Wark, Violet Baldock and Edith Camm. Sir Josiah was succeeded by Wilfred's brother, the Rt Hon Trevor Charles.

When the bomb fell on the 16 April 1941 near the end of Court Downs Rd, Gilbert Crease, one of the five sons of James Crease of 30 Wickham Rd, had been removing incendiaries from the roof of the house opposite, using long handled shovels. The bomb exploded as he was crossing back across the road. A piece of the smashed fire engine (see Ch 5) sliced off his foot and a bomb splinter broke the femur of the other leg! According to his son, David, he had a difficult twisted walk ever afterwards. Another of the five brothers, Percy, had received a severe head injury due to shrapnel from a bomb at the junction of Thicket Rd and Crystal Palace Park Rd on October 18 1940. It kept him in hospital until the 1 March 1941 and affected his sight and hearing. Ironically all five brothers had survived WWI all starting in the Kent Yeomanry, only for two of them to receive serious injuries as civilians in WWII.

Pamela Netherstreet describes her experiences of the night of 16 April. They had moved into Grosvenor Rd, West Wickham in February and it was arranged that Pamela would go to St David's College.

> *'The siren went about 9 pm and very soon the whole area was ringed with flares, a most amazing sight. An incendiary bomb landed at the bottom of the garden which was quickly dealt with and Mum and I took shelter in the cupboard under the stairs.*

*Uncle who hated being confined stayed in the kitchen. Auntie was on her way upstairs to the loo when Mum pushed her downstairs and came back to me. We didn't hear a thing when the bomb hit just a sensation of a lift rushing down. Right in front of us was a perfectly shaped tunnel but my leg was pinned down by a beams so I could not move. Mum was all right apart from a wound on her head. Gas was escaping so we put on our gas masks even though they were no good for coal gas! We called for help and the Home Guard came over as their station was only at the bottom of our garden. Corporal Thaw crawled down our tunnel and had an awful job removing the beam from my leg. Something hit him on the head but he carried on and was awarded a medal for his bravery that night. A Canadian soldier rescued Auntie from the downstairs loo but Uncle was badly crushed and it was some hours before he was rescued from the remnants of the kitchen. We had breakfast of bread, butter and strawberry jam in the church hall but I had a wasp in mine.*

*We moved to a flat in The Avenue, Beckenham. We loved Beckenham that was still called The Village with family run shops like Underwoods, the greengrocer on the corner of Manor Rd. The raids abated and Mum went to work at Muirheads making wireless sets for submarines and taking her part firewatching for which she was given a tin hat. After a year off school, I started at the Prendagast in Catford and things were quiet until the flying bombs.'*

Tony Johns whose uncle was Rob Copeland, tells of his experiences during the blitz and subsequently after returning from Limpsfield to where his school, Aske's, had been evacuated.

*'During my brief evacuation to Limpsfield in Surrey, my family had moved from Forest Ridge to a much larger house at 18 Bromley Rd on the opposite corner of Bevington Rd to the Methodist church. My bedroom was on the top floor with two windows, one facing the church and the other facing Manor Rd.*

*I had been home in bed for a few days with flu. On 20 January 1943, the day the Fokkerwulf 190 bombed and machine-gunned Sandhurst School at Catford, I heard the sound of low flying aircraft. I jumped out of bed just in time to see an ME 109 with a Spitfire on its tail fly between our house and the Methodist church. I could see both pilots clearly. Moving to the other window, I saw both aircraft climb to avoid the trees of Kelsey Park. I believe the German was shot down over open countryside.*

Tony Johns in 1946.

(Raiders had penetrated the Thames defences on 'scalded cat' raids but seven were destroyed, four ME 109s and three FW 190s. The one seen by Tony was probably the one that crashed at Capel in Surrey.)

Tony Johns today.

*Our house had a cellar where we slept at night on purpose-built beds and with the floor shored up above us which made us feel a lot safer. The cellar door was always left open in the day and our dog, 'Grip' could detect the difference between the sound of enemy aircraft and ours. Even before we could hear anything, he would warn us with a bark and was always down the cellar steps first.*

*During one of the dogfights over Beckenham at the beginning of September, I watched as a Hurricane was shot down by a Messerschmitt 109. I raced on my bike to find it had crashed on the golf course at Park Langley just off Wickham Way. The pilot had bailed out but the plane was burning furiously with ammunition exploding all around.*

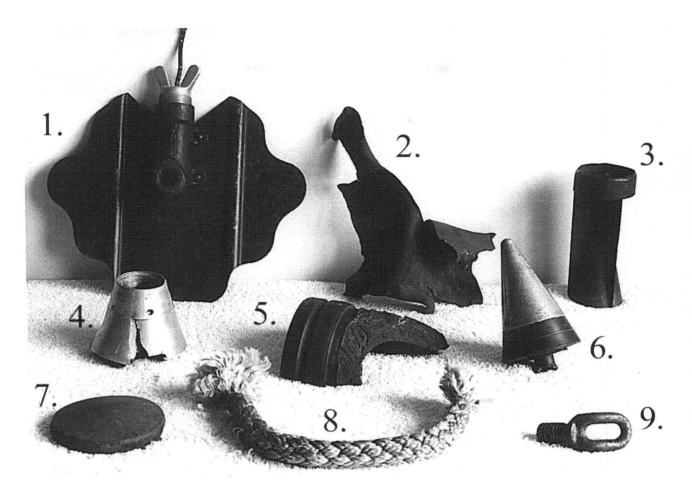

Tony Johns' Shrapnel Collection

1. End plate from Incendiary Bomb canister

2. Piece of casing from Oil Bomb (Regal Cinema)

3. Incendiary Bomb fin (from Pickhurst)

4. & 6. Two Anti Aircraft Shell nose caps and

5. Piece of Anti Aircraft Shell shrapnel (from Grandparents (the Copelands) garden in Bromley Road)

7. Base cap from Anti Aircraft Shell

8. Piece of Cord from Parachute Mine (Greenways)

9. Ring from High Explosive Bomb (Pickhurst)

*My collection of souvenirs includes a piece of AA shell shrapnel weighing 2.5 lbs that hit the roof of my grandparents house and fell in their garden in Bromley Rd. There is a piece of parachute cord from the Greenways landmine and a fin from an incendiary bomb. My cousin Michael Clark and I found nine or ten unexploded incendiaries in soft mud at Pickhurst and we cycled home with them strung from our handlebars like onion men. Michael's father, Arthur Clark, was an officer in the Home Guard and he knew a thing or two about these bombs. He removed the fins and end plugs so that we could empty out the thermite. We discharged the detonators by dropping the bombs from a bedroom window on to the concrete path below and then refitted the plugs and fins.*
*(Michael was killed in Holland shortly after his call up in 1944).*

*On another occasion we found a defused unexploded bomb in a field at Pickhurst and the ring which had supported the bomb in the bomb bay became part of my collection. We were always souvenir hunting after air raids never giving a thought to the fact that it could be our last day! I also added my father's AFS sleeping bag to my 'museum.' Many of our fathers were part time firemen, like Reg Leeks, my father, Rob Johns and Ted Nash. For a time I had a piece of a barrage balloon. It had come down in flames and draped what remained of itself over the roofs of the houses in The Drive, Beckenham, just down from Church Avenue.*

*Like many teenagers, I joined the ATC 386 Squadron held in Elm Rd. Sometimes our parents would consent to us going to the fighter station at Biggin Hill where we helped out in the armoury, the radio section or parachute packing. If the fighters were scrambled, we would lay in the long grass around the perimeter to count the aircraft back, giving the last one a cheer. I remember a very young pilot returning very low through the valley between Biggin Hill and Layhams Rd landing with twigs clipped from the tree tops. We had dinner in the airmen's mess, more often than not sausages, mashed potato and processed peas followed by suet pudding and golden syrup.*

*Towards the end of the day if all was quiet, we would be given a flight in a De Haviland 'Domine' a twin engined biplane which was the RAF version of the civilian 'Rapide.' Cycling home from school one Friday afternoon I met a chauffeur driven black car held up by the traffic lights at Manor Rd. Sitting in the back seat was Winston Churchill on his way home to Chartwell from Downing St. A few weeks later when exactly the same thing happened I gave him a Victory 'V' salute, hoping that my hand was the right way round.*

(Another resident, Mrs Durling, was thrilled to see the Prime Minister's car take a short cut through Goddard Rd as he returned to his home in Kent.)

The account above by Tony Johns of the surprise attack on 20 January 1943 is confirmed by Mrs S. She was in the kitchen of her flat on the first floor of 11 Wheatsheaf Parade on the corner of West Wickham High Street and Surrey Road which curved and widened at this point. She saw the approaching German plane skimming the roof tops of nearby houses and when it reached her it was level with her kitchen. The pilot was looking at her and *'his eyes looked right through me'*, she recalls.

Having survived a bomb attack in 1941 on her previous home in Epsom, inappropriately called 'Worlds End', Mrs S was able to brush off this second skirmish with the enemy, even though it took place a few days before the birth of her fourth child on 27th January 1943.

In Epsom, her two elder children had slept right through the night, being saved from injury, when a huge window crashed on their bed, by the thick curtains that contained the glass. Indeed they remained fast asleep even when the ARP wardens carefully lifted the debris off the bed. After that episode, Mrs S vowed that she would never go in a shelter:

*'If we have to go, I will prefer to be above ground not below it'.*

The war was never far from Mrs S in West Wickham. Her husband was in the AFS based at the fire station in Glebe Way. Just beyond the station there were tank traps - great blocks of concrete - because it was thought that if there ever was an invasion that was the route that the Germans would take. In fact, Mrs S. recalls that very few people ever expected an invasion and the main concern was the air raids.

# Four
# Evacuation, Education, Excitement

What has happened to my life; why am I here?
Where's my best friend and my dog, Rover, so dear?
I long for my Dad and my field where to roam
What is this thing 'war' that has torn me from home?
At ten years old just put on a train
Brother stands waving, will I see you again?
I stand popping fuchsias, can't keep back a tear
For my Rover, my rabbits and chickens; not here.

Pat Manning

Evacuation was not offered at first to any of the residents of Beckenham because the town was sufficiently far from the centre of London to be thought safe. If you went to a London school however, you could find yourself carried off to the countryside even though you lived in Beckenham. The experience of Pat Manning follows:

'We had been in Poundfield Hall, Green Lane, Jarvis Brook, Sussex since dinner time on 1 September 1939 and the ladies were clearing up. Edna Ely and I had watched all the other children leave for their foster homes and no one wanted us so we hoped that we were going back home.

We were evacuees from Haseltine Rd School, Bell Green, Lower Sydenham, SE26. Earlier in the day we had boarded a steam train for an unknown destination and ended up at Jarvis Brook station in East Sussex. We walked in a crocodile from the station down in the valley until we were halfway up the hill to Crowborough when we turned off at Green Lane.

Now it was five o'clock and as we piled into the back of a car and headed back along the lane we couldn't wait to catch the steam train back to London. On the way we stopped at what seemed to be a church and we were told to knock on the door.

We weren't going home but were being billeted at the Rest House of Lady Trevor!

Pat Manning

17

*Apart from the tiny lady dressed in black with a lacy mantilla over her white hair, there was the tall housekeeper, Miss Hadley and a young woman who was Lady Trevor's companion. We were taken up the centre staircase to a room immediately above the front door and told that we were NEVER to go to the West wing of the house which was Lady Trevor's.*

*Next door to us was the companion (soon to disappear into the land Army), then the sewing maid and opposite, the dragon, Miss Hadley. Round in the East wing were the servants, Louisa the parlour maid, Alice the house maid, the little kitchen maid and Cook who was never known by any other name. The chauffeur slept over the stables to complete the household of nine people. That is how I came to have a National registration card of EKPB 102 11 because with Edna slightly older, I was the eleventh in the house.*
*We ate with the servants. To this day there are many foods that I cannot swallow. I was given a plate piled with liver, carrots, swedes, potatoes and boiled rice when I had the appetite of a sparrow and would have been happy with a sausage and cabbage with gravy. I wrote pathetic letters home and my parents visited leaving a long line of carrier bags full of food (I remember tins of sardines) in the servants' quarters. Then Lady Trevor came in and was truly horrified at the impression that she was not feeding the evacuees properly. Worse still, when Edna and I went up to our room, we found the floor covered with white sailcloth because my ink bottle had leaked on to the carpet.*

*Two things fascinated me in this house. In the entrance hall, there was a model garden constructed from mosses of all kinds with a mirror for a pond. Ten years later at Imperial College studying for an Honours degree in Botany I was able to give names to all those mosses, liverworts too. Then every evening, we were invited into the drawing room to listen to the companion playing the grand piano and to play with a wonderful compendium of games fitted into a wooden casket.*

*Lady Trevor died after Christmas and I was rebilleted with a rose grower, his wife and toddler which really suited me far more but I've never forgotten the mysterious Lady who lived in the forbidden West wing with whom I played board games.'*

Many Beckenham residents left at their own expense and this included several of the private schools such as Minshull House from Park Rd that shut for the duration of the war. They started out from Waterloo on a specially scheduled train, assorted children with gasmasks hanging from their shoulders in cardboard boxes, each child with a small suitcase. They were struck by the beauty of miles of sand as they arrived at Woolacombe in Devon. They stayed at a hotel called Combes Hotel which is still there today called The Royal Hotel. They had 23 children in their care that included some boys from Beckenham's Clare House. The hotel had been a summer residence only and had no central heating so it was very cold in the bitterly cold war time winters.

Beckenham's Minshull House was kept occupied and the school hall was used for a while for the meetings of the Sea Cadets when they were bombed out of Copers Cope Rd. Clare House joined with the Abbey School and went to the South coast.

Although evacuation was not an option, the Beckenham children were not allowed to attend schools until air raid shelters had been provided. An alternative was to hold small classes in private homes and school pavilions so that large numbers of children were not assembled in the same place. Eventually evacuation was provided for children on the west side of the Lower Sydenham to Elmers End railway line from January 1941.

One third of the school population of Penge, 600 children, left from Waterloo for Exmouth or Exeter on 2 January but fewer than 200 Beckenham children went from Paddington to Neath. Only Stewart Fleming, Churchfields, Alexandra and the two County schools were eligible from the Beckenham schools.

The Beckenham Borough Council continued to urge the Ministry to declare the whole of Beckenham an evacuation area because all the children from Balgowan, Marian Vian, Hawes Down and Bromley Rd areas were not eligible. John Blundell who started at the Beckenham & Penge County School for Boys in 1939 recalls that when approximately half the boys were evacuated the remainder were put on a rota so that they were never all under the same roof. One group would be at the Tablonians Sports Pavilion, another at Park Langley, a third at the Penge Congregational church, lessons in the main school would be in ground floor rooms and periodically they would have work set to do at home.

William Duckworth was another Beckenham boy who stayed put for nearly all of the war. It didn't matter that schooling was interrupted. He didn't want to be evacuated. He lived in Beckenham Rd over an off-licence. He describes an experience when he was about 11 as follows.

> 'I was inside looking out of the window when a sneak raider flew by down Beckenham Rd going towards Crystal Palace. Mum noticed it first. She heard the engine or machine gun and said "Get down." A bullet went through my Mum's bedroom window and ended up in her wardrobe. Rudlands, the shop next door, had a cannon shell in the brickwork. When I went to school I told the other children "Look what happened to me" and no doubt exaggerated it, turning one plane into two!'

Many families in Beckenham departed by their own choice. As the blitz was building up, Edna Antrobus, pregnant with her second child, went to Cirencester with her three year old daughter, Celia (Wookey). Her husband, Harvey, employed by the Wellcome Foundation at Langley Court, chose Cirencester as the only place that was not teeming with evacuees but on arrival they found their luggage had been left at Paddington station and they could find nowhere to stay. When Edna tried to book up at the only maternity home she was told that they were fully booked until March and the baby was due on 29 October! Little Yvonne, always known as Bobsa, arrived three days late at the Sunnyside Maternity Home, Cheltenham. She was nine months old before she entered her own house in Beckenham in August 1941.

Mollie Russell Smith moved from Tunbridge Wells to Beckenham in 1935 at age 13. She enjoyed art at evening classes and started full time studies at the Beckenham School of Art in Beckenham Road next to the Library in 1937.

In 1940, Mollie was living at 31 Cromwell Road when a bomb fell on Forster Road badly damaging adjacent properties and leaving a vast crater. Her house in Cromwell Road was protected from the blast by the mature trees. Nonetheless she was evacuated to Hadleigh near Ipswich where she joined a small Art School in Benton End.

There she met portrait painter, Lucian Freud, who was so impressed by her talent that he helped her enrol free of fees. She spent the next three years at Benton End before returning to Beckenham in 1943.

Mollie Russell Smith (MR)

In Essex her reserved occupation was nursery teaching but on her return to Beckenham she was told to report to Creed, a Croydon company, where she was employed on secret work developing new aiming equipment for RAF bombers.

A lot is written about evacuation at the beginning of the war and during the blitz but the V weapons caused another period of evacuation for the children of Beckenham and Penge in July 1944.

Jack Hilton tells of his evacuation to Lundwood, near Barnsley, South Yorkshire.

> 'We seemed to take forever to reach our destination, Barnsley, a mining town in Yorkshire. After the night at the civic centre, everyone was taken to their new homes until there were only me and my two friends left. Then we were taken in a closed van to our unknown destination and when my friends got out I had never felt so lonely in all my life. The next stop was to be my new home, 56 Wyke Rd.

Jack Hilton and parents (JH)                    Jack Hilton and Mr and Mrs Wines (JH)

*'The driver knocked at the side door (they never used the front doors) and a lady with a little girl answered. She was Mrs Wines, my wartime Mum to be. "It was a boy you wanted," said the driver, "Sign here please." It appears that she had been asked in 1939 if she would take an evacuee in the event of war and five years later I turned up! She gave me corned beef, new potatoes, tomatoes and pickles, a meal I relish to this day. She spoke with an accent I had a job to understand and when her husband came home from the pit she had some explaining to do as to what this thirteen year old boy was doing there. My wartime Mum and I gelled immediately. We got on famously.*

*She was my substitute Mum, best friend, my pal, everything. I was the son she never had. When I went to the Barnsley Central school and was made a prefect she was so proud. After about a month, we went to Blackpool for a holiday which seemed completely untouched by war. While we were there my mother died. My world collapsed and I had to get back to my little brother. My father who had been called up when he was 42 could easily be killed in France as could my brother in London with the doodlebugs.*

*Thirty years were to pass before I made my way back to my war time Mum, returning several times with my family after that, sitting with Mrs Wines by the fire, just chatting.'*

Yvonne Fish was another evacuee sent to Yorkshire to escape the doodlebugs. She was a pupil at the Beckenham County School for Girls who departed in the middle of July from Kings Cross station bound for Doncaster.

*'Many of us decided to join the evacuation party because we thought Yorkshire sounded a good place for a holiday. When we arrived, several of us aged 15 years or so, the mining community thought we should be at work. The villages had been expecting 5 year olds not great gallumping teenagers! Evacuees had the reputation for being 'lousy, bedwetters from the city slums' not middle class Beckenham young ladies. We finally arrived at Goldthorpe where we were gathered in the school hall while the local folk came to look us over. My brother and I had promised that we would not be separated and as nobody wanted to take us, the kindly WVS ladies took us to the next village of Thurnscoe where, sad and bedraggled, we were taken in by Mr and Mrs Lunn..*

*Things were never the same again. We learned the local dialect. We got used to mushy peas and chips for supper. We went pea picking in the rain to try to earn some pocket money. We experienced a mega culture shock to discover how a miner's family lived. I began to notice that when I went to bed, the sheets were warm and gritty. Mr Lunn was on night shifts at the Pit so it appeared he was using my bed during the day! We discovered the really deep snow of a Yorkshire winter. We went to Wath-on-Dearne Grammar School and found out what it was like to be taught in a mixed class where the girls were expected to sit at the back and let the boys take over.*

*However we grew close to our teachers and slowly appreciated that this rough place in Yorkshire had its own particular kind of hospitality.'*

Lewis Blake who attended LCC schools during the war considered that he only received two years of uninterrupted education during the war in 1942 and 1943 and that, as a result, by the end of 1944, half the 13 year olds at his school were illiterate. There is another side to the story though. The authorities cut the school holidays to a week or so at Christmas and Easter with three only weeks in the summer. Also, since teaching was a reserved occupation, many of us had the same teachers throughout our time at school. Few can say that is the case today. The teachers stayed after school for games like evening tennis and came in on Saturday mornings for our matches. They produced Gilbert & Sullivan comic operas and ran drama and musical societies. Our teachers did their best to make our lives as normal as possible and it is a great credit to them that they succeeded.

The Beckenham and Penge County School boys had their own school flight (578) of the Air Training Corps where the boys learned the basics of Morse code, aircraft recognition, rifle training and square bashing and a Fairey battle bomber was placed on the far side of the school grounds. Those who went on to serve in the RAF were grateful for their ATC training.

Douglas Smith started at the County School from Bromley Rd at the same time as John Blundell and remembers how his school career was set back about a month while shelters were being constructed and brick walls built to make the gym as safe as possible. He was not evacuated either. His father was an air raid warden complete with armband and a steel helmet with ARP on it and with duties such as fire-watching and handling a stirrup pump. Douglas knew the family in Greenways who were wiped out by the parachute mine and was shocked to see the property blown to smithereens. When the family received their Morrison shelter, his father slept on the top of it because he found it too claustrophobic to sleep underneath with four or five others! Once when he was visiting a friend with his mother, they thought that his father's business had received a direct hit but someone else had suffered that time. Douglas walked into the storeroom to find his father and found him in a daze as he had been hit on the head by a tin of paint. Cycling to their allotment in Copers Cope Rd, they heard a V1 which then cut out. When it exploded they found they had jumped off their bikes and landed in someone's front garden! Once or twice from school they went to help the Kent fruit farmers picking plums and wielding pitchforks to make haystacks. Douglas remembers trying Kent cider, just once, because his resulting headache was terrible and the room would just not keep still. He found out years later when he read an obituary in the Daily Telegraph that one of his teachers, Harry Raé who taught French, had been an undercover British agent who went to France in the war. In general, Douglas reckoned that life in school went on pretty normally in spite of the various incidents mentioned. Sports kept going very well, rugby, tennis, hockey and cricket with regular matches against other schools.

Greenways
landmine 1940 (MC)

Exciting opportunities came the way of many of the children who were evacuated. Carey Blyton was evacuated to West Lydford after he was bombed out of The Drive in July 1944 and he described the two months there as the most extraordinary of his life. He stayed at the Rectory, a large rambling house with the River Bure bordering the front lawn. He would swim with the dozens of minnows and eels in the deep water by the house. Below the bridge he caught trout among the chub, dace, roach, gudgeon and Miller's Thumb. He discovered the chrysalises of moths, butterflies and lacewings in the vegetation by the river and spent many an hour lifting up stones for water shrimps, caddis larvae and water scorpions. At dusk the bats would flit across the surface of the river and he saw his first field mice, slow-worm and lizards. He would catch rainbow trout for his mother using grasshoppers caught in the long grass, wriggling to the head of the pond where the fish lay in wait. He watched in a kind of horrified stupor as the first eel that he caught twisted itself into knots and covered everything with a thick jelly-like slime, eventually biting through the line.

Carey Blyton (CW)

Cliff Watkins was evacuated three times during WW2. His experiences follow:

*'I was born in Camberwell in May 1939 and a few months later my father George Watkins joined the Royal Engineers as a blacksmith. My mother, Annie, elder sister, Babs, older brother Bud (Roy) and I went to stay in a house in Watchbell Street in Rye, some 60 miles nearer the enemy!*

*The onset of the blitz led to my second evacuation to Nettlebed, near Oxford, where my family, sometimes including my paternal grandparents, lived in a bothy, reached by a frequently muddy farm track off the High Street. My first encounter with country life was the huge face of a cow peering through my bedroom window.*

*When the bombing in London seemed to be at an end, my family returned to a rented house at 90 Wiverton Road, on the Beckenham border. In 1944 the blast from a doodlebug (perhaps the one that destroyed Doris Pullen's house round the corner in Newlands Park} brought the kitchen window crashing onto the roof of the Morrison shelter. Soon we were back in the bothy, our home until the end of the war.*

*Now aged 5, the country became my adventure playground which included visits to the loo at the end of the garden. I, with my charge, my younger brother Tony, had freedom to roam the fields of Smiley's farm trying to avoid losing our wellies in the cowpats, One day, I was about to crawl through a gap in the hedgerow when I was confronted by a huge pig and made a rapid retreat.*

*Muck spreading saw me in the driving seat of a tractor, desperately trying to steady the wheel while the farmer, Mr Smiley tossed manure from the cart that the tractor was pulling.*

*The war time ambience was provided by a barrage balloon and camps for US troops massing for D Day. The POW's in their camps seemed to me like zoo animals who spent all day peering at me from their cages. My own freedom took its toll when I managed to decapitate a finger investigating the mechanics of a bicycle chain!*

*I visited Nettlebed in 2004 with my wife Veronica. We discovered that the bothy (see left) was still inhabited and we exchanged wartime memories with a Mr Clark, tending the church graveyard. He was born in the village in 1929 and had plenty of tales to tell.' (CW)*

Veronica Watkins (nee Jones) recalls - A toddler's view of the war:

Veronica and her mother Marian (VW)

*I was born in September 1942 so my memories are few, but very clear. My parents lived at that time in Thicket Road, Penge, in the ground floor flat of a converted Victorian house. 'The Blackout', to me, meant the long, heavy curtains which hung at the kitchen and bedroom windows. Those were the rooms in which we spent most of our hours as a family. 'Blackout' had no other significance and I thought it was the name of the material.*

*One evening, when it was bedtime for my elder brother and me, my parents carried our beds into the big kitchen so that we would 'feel safe'. I was a bit puzzled at this since I was far more frightened of a telling-off from my father than I was of the mystery that was called 'war'.*

*At some point my mother took us off for a private evacuation. I think I remember this so well because it was an intriguing happening in my hitherto small world. We went by train and I sat on my mother's lap and thought the carriage was magic with its thick leather strap to raise and lower the window and its shiny lacquered wood. We were travelling to Leeds, not a good choice since it was bombed - although probably not at that time - but my father had family there. When we arrived we stayed in a house which had steps up to the front door and no front garden. We were put into a long, narrow room where my brother and I had to share a single bed: me at the top end and he at the bottom. I took a dim view of this and was even less pleased when we got the measles and had to spend all day in it. A doctor was called, my mother took off my liberty bodice and the doctor sat me on his knee and listened to my chest with his stethoscope. At this point the lady of the house and her son stuck their heads round the door to check what was going on. I thought this a terrible intrusion, and deliberately set up an almighty wail at which they decamped with speed.*

*At breakfast our evacuation hosts complained constantly about a large black dog which kept knocking over the milk bottles left by the milkman at the bottom of the front steps. Shortages of food and difficulties of rationing made this more than just irritating. I didn't ever see the dog but imagined it as something of a monster.*

*We didn't stay long in Leeds. Even at my young age I felt the people in the house hadn't really wanted us there. Added to that my mother was rarely able to visit the family from whom she'd hoped to get moral support, and so back we came to Penge.*

*Other memories are necessarily stories which were related to me by my parents. One such told how, on the way back from a visit to the dentist, my mother was blown in through a shop window by bomb blast up near the Crystal Palace and, amazingly unhurt, rushed home to my grandmother's, where Mum had left me and my brother. We'd been playing next to a conservatory and she found her son covered from head to foot in dust, standing stock-still with shock, and her daughter with a mouth full of glass. The glass wasn't swallowed and the dust could be washed, so all was well. I have to say I remember nothing of this. Other tales were of my father who, on his way home from Home Guard duty in the blackout, walked into a wall and broke most of his upper teeth. He was an electronics engineer, which was a reserved occupation, and he worked at times with the Navy. Recently I found a Pass issued in his name which allowed him to work for a month at RAF Station, Turnberry. The reason for the Pass, it states, was 'Employment (M.A.P.)' I don't know what the letters stand for but he was put up in Beresford Hotel in Ayr, which must have made a nice change from poor battered Penge.*

# Five
# Fortress Beckenham

When a raid was in progress it could be very noisy. Anti-aircraft shells exploding overhead, the whistle of falling shrapnel, exploding bombs, incendiaries, searchlights and flares across the sky as well as the drone of planes. I didn't go to bed for ninety consecutive nights during the 1940/41 blitz. It was work during the day and Civil Defence Duty at night.

E J Pouelsen

Fortress Beckenham defended the South Eastern approaches to London and protected local people from the worst effects of the weapons of war, its citizen soldiers augmented by regular British forces and prisonesr of war.

Guns, searchlights, projectors, predictors, troops, trenches, air raid shelters, barrage balloons, sandbags, shrapnel, thousands of local people in uniform, parades, soldiers and armaments on the trains, tracks defended by pill boxes were aspects of everyday life in Fortress Beckenham.

## THE HOME GUARD
On 14 May 1940, Eden broadcast an appeal for 250,000 men to enrol as a citizen army. Nearly two million responded 'clamouring for weapons and uniforms, and demanding to be drilled and trained.' Identified only by an armlet with the letters LDV (Local Defence Volunteers), they were unpaid, met their own expenses and often paid for their equipment and uniforms. They created their own weapons and defences; the two old coal carts tethered to the ground by huge wooden stakes and chains seen by ten year old Jack Hilton in Alexandra Park being typical.

William Jones (2nd right, back row) in The Home Guard, Anerley Z Battery (VW)

Gradually they were supplied with weapons and uniforms and organised along similar lines to the regular army. Then on 14 July Churchill gave them the name 'Home Guard' and the threat that they would 'fight on the beaches, the landing grounds and the house tops' was a factor considered by the Germans when they decided on the bombing blitz on London and other cities rather than a land invasion.

## The Home Guard Z Batteries

By 1942 some units of the Home Guard were sub-divided into G.S. (General Service) Battalions and A.A. (Anti Aircraft) Batteries. The latter were under the command of the Regular Army although they still 'belonged' to a local Home Guard G.S. Battalion.

As well as Ack Ack guns a lesser known weapon was used by the anti-aircraft ground defences - multiple rocket launchers. Trials started in 1939 and around the country by the end of 1941 there were nearly 2,000 projectors, the official name for the launch cradles. These held two rows of rockets which could reach 19,000 feet.

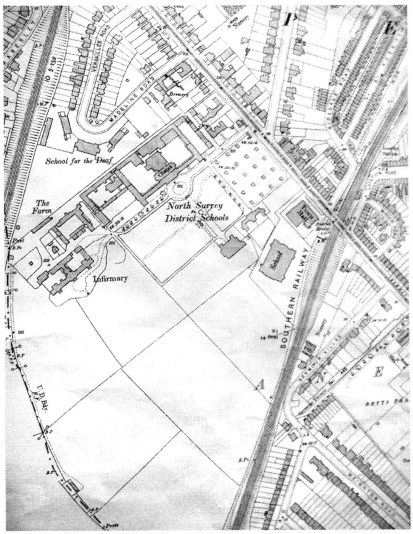

Site of the 'Z' Rocket AA Battery west of Anerley Town Hall. (BL)

The projectors were operated by two men under radar control. 16 rockets were fired from each projector - 8 on each side.

## The Anerley Z Battery

In October 1942 the 101 Surrey Home Guard Rocket Anti Aircraft Battery (projectors, radar cabins etc,) was established on a triangular site in Penge which had been used for 3.7 A.A. guns by the regular army adjacent to Anerley Town Hall. Use was made by the Z battery of the available buildings, previously a small boys school, a workhouse and part of the North Surrey Schools complex (see map). Some 1,300 men and women were stationed there, including 50 officers.

Local volunteers for this new battery were transferred from 'D' Company of the 57 London Battalion which operated as the Penge Company of the Home Guard. Additionally, civilian men in reserve occupations were diverted there by the local National Service Organisations, as was the case of William Jones who moved to Thicket Road, Penge in 1942.

Life could be hazardous. A projector was controlled by one man inside its central body and fired by the man using foot pedals. Operation of one pedal only resulted in one side launching causing the apparatus to whizz round on a vertical axis, rather like a Katherine wheel. As the projectors had been built with only half the required space between them to fit into the Anerley site, being near any of them when they were fired was hazardous. William Jones spoke of spinning cables whipping mens feet from under them.

64 projectors were located at Anerley although manning meant that a maximum of just 48 were ever used. But this meant that almost 1,000 rockets could be launched at once creating a formidable defence screen against enemy raids on London.

## Other Home Guard Units

By 1942, the Beckenham and West Wickham Battalion was called the 55th West Kent Home Guard. By 1942, its P Zone Commander, Col Chamberlain, was confident that they were ready to repel any invasion from the air. They had regular weekend training camps on the 100 acre former Boy Scouts site in Kent and had recently acquired an AA battery that was encouraging the uptake of young recruits of 17 years. They had a cadet force training boys from 14 to 17 and there were plenty of openings at the other end of the scale for drivers and motorcyclists over military age. The Mayor and Col Chamberlain inspected the Home Guard at the Abbey Field, Brackley Rd in March 1942 where there was an impressive and realistic afternoon of displays such as unarmed combat and machine gun warfare.

55th Battalion Kent House Guard, August 1940
Inspection by George VI at Glebe House, West Wickham
(BL)

Together with the Heavy and Light Rescue squads, the AFS and Wardens service, the Home Guard was immediately on the scene of any incident to rescue the trapped and injured with assistance from a mobile medical unit run by Dr Edden. Various First Aid Posts were located all over the borough such as the Town Hall where Tony Bristow's mother was a nurse and the Swimming Baths in Beckenham Rd.

A tragedy occurred on 2 March 1942 at the Home Guard training ground at Skid Hill (now the site of Fairchildes High School, New Addington.) Twelve year old boys Kenneth Dailey, Alexander Baker, Roland Fothergill and Allan Wilkins from Layham's Rd were all killed when one of four trench mortar shells they had picked up exploded. The shells were with 15 unexploded smoke bombs that they thought could do them no harm. There were no warning notices at the site which was easy to access through a stranded wire fence. This incident was especially sad since there were no raids on Beckenham at all in 1942.

War Weapons Week in Beckenham High Street 1941
(SC)

## The ARP WARDENS

The backbone of fortress Beckenham was the 1,200 men and women who served in the sixty ARP posts. EJ Pouelsen's ARP Post 34 was purpose built, 8ft x 4ft. Facing the door was a table with telephone, log-book and record book with a clock on the wall behind. On each side was a bench convertible into a bunk bed. Tea making equipment and emergency rations were on a shelf over one of the seats and on the opposite wall was a map of the area, neighbouring posts with telephone numbers.

55th Battalion Kent Home Guard, August 1940
Inspection by George VI at Glebe House, West Wickham
(BL)

ARP POST 28
VAILE'S GARAGE BECKENHAM.

(SC)

A household register listed names and addresses with shelter arrangements, number in the house and next of kin. If householders were away, they entrusted us with their keys. In a shed outside was gas clothing for all the wardens, picks, shovels, rope, signs, oil lamps, debris baskets and a chemical toilet.

The night personnel consisted of

A Post Warden in command

Deputy Post Warden

Assistant Post Warden

18 Wardens in 3 groups on duty every third night unless there were many incidents.

At first we only had an ARP armband with a blue boiler suit, steel helmet and gasmask. Later in September 1941 when the Civil Defence was created, we had a blue battledress and army boots as well and the wardens were provided with blankets since most were part time and worked elsewhere during the day. As incendiaries became more elaborate, long handled shovels were added to the regulation stirrup pump and those fighting fires were urged to shield themselves with something like a dustbin lid to protect from explosions.

Duties included fitting and testing gasmasks, checking the public shelters, giving advice and keeping the household register up to date as well as checking the blackout was secure.

Mayor William Sampson in his capacity of Chief ARP warden at the Town Hall Post 39. (SC)

Part of the communication links between the ARP Posts was provided by the Scout Messenger Service provided by teenage boys carrying messages on their bicycles. One of their number was Harold Tatman who lived at Elmers End at the corner of Goddard and Croydon Rd. There was an air raid siren was next to the police box right outside his house. Another Messenger was Neil Weiss the older son of Francis Weiss who feared for Neil when he was out during an air raid.

Next to the firemen's memorial is one to the Wardens and Heavy Rescue men who died at four separate incidents. It was unveiled on 20 October 1946 by Mayor Guy Brooks. The Heavy Rescue men were all laid to rest at this grave but the Wardens are elsewhere, Gladys Blinkhorn-Hay and Leslie Hurst of Post 40 in area S9 and the Florence and Reginald Seath of Post 42 at Faversham cemetery.

The Beckenham Borough Council bought a piece of land where Post 40 was by St Marks School, Queen Anne Ave and placed a plaque there in memory of all the Air Raid wardens who died in the war.

# THE GUNS AND SEARCHLIGHTS

The anti-aircraft multiple rocket launchers at Anerley was just one of the many sites on which guns were located all over Beckenham. The light AA Bofors guns, which fired almost vertically, were mounted on railway wagons and transported up and down the Victoria line through Beckenham Junction station. They made a distinctive sound distinguishing them from the other guns in the district. Four Ack Ack guns were permanently placed at the Elgood playing fields protected by a deep trench round the perimeter. In 1939 the whole of the field had been covered with wire netting spread over two feet high brick columns with the gun emplacement in the middle. This did not prevent Tony Bristow getting in there and coming home with a trophy, a two foot tall shell case.

He was one of the T.S. Sikh Sea Cadets moved from place to place when their HQ in Copers Cope Rd was demolished by a bomb and the Elgood pavilion was one of the places where they were temporarily housed. Other people report guns on the land behind Overbury Avenue and at the cricket ground in Foxgrove Rd.

Francis Weiss junior reports 'An Anti Aircraft Battery was placed in the field behind 24 Overbury Avenue and the house next door to us became the Officer's Mess. I had pretty well absolute freedom to play in the mess, and on the guns! When the officers had a party, they borrowed all my mother's china and cutlery for the occasion.'

The real purpose of gunfire was not to shoot down enemy planes although plenty were destroyed by the gunners. Their main function was to keep the enemy so high in the air that he could not see the target and was deterred from flying straight enough for accurate bombing. The AA gunfire also attracted the fighters into the area to shoot down the enemy.

Searchlights remembered by contributors include those by the AA guns at the Ella sports ground in Worsley Bridge Rd near where the river Pool goes beneath the road. Many people recall the beams sweeping across the sky and little Hazel Cummings (now Jean Bogle) remembers being very frightened when she was caught in in a searchlight sweeping across the pavement in Eden Park Avenue.

Robert Sawyer's picture of barrage balloons over Penge in 1940. Taken from the Beccehamian (AH1)

# To a barrage balloon
(from the Beccehamian 1939)

HEIL to thee blithe bladder,
Bird thou never wert;
Doth hydrogen or badder
Gases fill thy heart
I pray thou wilt not unpremeditated part,

Like a high-born Goring
In his Sunday best,
So adiposely purring
Over a secret chest,
With all the medals filled which overflow his breast.

Like a silver sorsage
In a Frankfurt stew
Dangling from thy corsage
Of aerial hue
A cable from a lorry screened from vulgar view.

We look before and after
And pine for what is not,
How can this be the craft ter
Do what we think it ought?
How can thy portly bulk with deadliness be fraught?

# BARRAGE BALLOONS

Barrage balloons were part of the defensive roof over our town. The RAF Balloon Command was responsible for controlling huge silver balloons which held up cables strong enough to destroy any aircraft colliding with them. Not that it was their defined function. Their purpose was to prevent low level flights, strafing and dive bombing. Many of us can remember times when the balloons were grounded and we were machine gunned by lone aircraft. Peter Forster was looking out of an upstairs window of 78 Goddard Rd when he and his sister spotted a JU88 coming towards them. Their father was parading with the Home Guard at Marian Vian School and the pilot dropped his bombs. Fortunately he must have spotted them too late as the bomb load exploded harmlessly near Green View Avenue off the Glade. Both Marian Vian and the Beckenham County School for Girls in Lennard Rd were machine gunned across the playgrounds, luckily with no casualties.

Beckenham's balloons were grouped closely together. For example there was one in Lloyds Bank ground in Copers Cope Rd, another over Cator Park and Cyphers Sports Ground, a third where the Alexandra Junior School was built in 1954, a fourth in the Penge Recreation ground opposite St John's Church and a fifth in Beckenham Place Park on the high ground in front of the mansion. From 1941, they were handled by the WAAF and would be put up in minutes when the siren went. Occasionally shot down in flames by enemy fighters, the crew would immediately set to inflating a replacement. In high winds the balloons had to be anchored nose to wind by 56 pound concrete blocks to keep the lethal cable under control.

Tony Johns remembers one that came down in flames and draped itself over the rooftops of the houses in The Drive by Church Avenue with its cable along the road. Escaped balloons were not uncommon and he saw two ancient Gloster Gladiators shoot one down over Limpsfield.

Barrage balloons were originally used in the First World War but by 1936 the Air Staff were planning how to site them for maximum effect in the future. They experimented with the idea of a circle round London but abandoned that in favour of balloons dotted all over the area to keep attacking planes high in the air.

The next question was to what height a balloon could lift not only its own weight but that of the heavy cable. It was decided on a medium height that would prevent accurate bomb aiming and dive bombing by the enemy.

Finally territorial balloon squadrons were organised round a nucleus of regular personnel which could be deployed in the event of war. Early in 1938, the London balloon squadrons were recruited and performance was so satisfactory that in 1939 barrages were developed for all major cities. On the first day of WW2, the London barrage was more or less complete and by 1940 there were thousands flying over Britain. They were vulnerable to storms and a number were destroyed by lightning on Friday afternoon 13 September 1939. Two fell in flames on two Beckenham houses and their cables damaged the roofs. The barrage stayed down on Saturday for the first time since the war began but they were all back in their defensive positions over London the next day.

Crews and public christened their balloons and, when the WAAFs took over in January 1941, the names took a romantic turn with 'Romeo' rather than 'Annie' or 'Matilda.' It took 16 airwomen to do the work of 10 airmen but the many modifications in the equipment enabled the women to operate the balloons where previously men's physical strength had been needed.

The balloon is a streamlined rubber proofed cotton bag about 63ft long and 31 ft high. It weighs about 550lbs and is flown on a flexible steel cable. Filled with hydrogen, it takes about 20 minutes to rise and the three fins keep it riding head-on to the wind. To see a flotilla of silver balloons flying as the sun went down was indeed a comforting sight for the population.

# TRENCHES AND AIR RAID SHELTERS

The air raid shelters provided at the Girls County School in Lennard Road were little more than WW1 style trenches dug on the playing field. Like the familiar images of WW1, they soon filled up with water and duckboards proved ineffective. Stoically the girls used them as commanded by the headmistress, Miss Fox. She put in the school log for 24 September that she had called for the Royal Engineers to attend to unexploded bombs which had fallen in the trenches.

Geoffrey Crabb tells us about the shelters at Elmers End where his family took refuge.

*'Some time after our arrival at Elmers End, our Anderson shelters were delivered. The neighbours got together to help each other dig a large hole in the tough London clay, bolt together the sheets of corrugated iron and then to cover the structure with the soil from the hole. But the clay had the last word because ours immediately filled with water to a depth of a couple of feet. When the council came along to line it with concrete, another six inches of water were added. I don't recall ever using it but our neighbour's shelter, the Louch family, was completely dry and I was to spend many hours in it later on in the war at the time of the flying bombs.*

*When the bombing started we used the Twinlock's shelter where my father had worked since 1922. On the other side of Elmers End station, the firm had bought the land to turn into a sports field but at the outbreak of war had built a number of shelters with allotments over the top. We collected bedding and other overnight stuff, traipsed down Eden Rd and over the railway bridge to spend the night in rather dank conditions. There were no bunks but merely planking where we slept side by side like fish on a slab. When we emerged in the morning it was to a different smell, that of the sewage farm that adjoined the site.*

Arriving home one night in the dark, Harold Tatman found that his front gate had gone and a burly, grim faced warden stopped him with the news that there was an unexploded 500lb bomb under the house. He found his parents at the Elmers End Free Church where they stayed for the next 10 days or so until the bomb was removed.

Jean Bogle, aka Hazel Cummings remembers the council surface shelter by 101 Eden Park Ave where she spent many 'scary nights' The shelter was dimly lit and heated by a primus stove at one end. Those not in the public shelters found the safest place at home was under the staircase. Three year old Brenda Banks at 17 Thayers Farm Road was saved in a house where only the party wall and the stairs were left standing.

By contrast, Olive Rippengal's father constructed a concrete shelter in the back garden of their home in Upper Elmers Road, still there today although filled with water.

A modern day "shelter" for the elderly is at Bencurtis Park, where the Glebe Housing Association West Wickham has provided housing for the elderly. This was originally the home of High Sheriff, Francis Walter Chamberlain, solicitor and the Home Guard 'P' Zone Commander during the war. The house was bequeathed for use by retired people by his wife Mrs Chamberlain.

Olive Rippengal's concrete shelter. (PM)

## REGULAR TROOPS

The barrage balloons were operated or supervised by regular RAF personnel like those at the IBIS sports ground off Cator Road. The RAC manned the AA battery by Overbury Avenue. Canadians were billeted in Copers Cope Road. The top of Crystal Palace Park was used by the Royal Army Service Corps and was a NO GO area for the public. Among other troops stationed there were the Gurkhas.

## TRAINS

The railway lines through Beckenham were supply lines for troops and arms going to the Kent ports. They were protected by pill boxes like the one that can still be seen by Bridge Road at a vital connection between the Victoria and Mid-Kent lines. The tracks were useful for moving big guns around like the huge naval guns nick-named the Boche Busters, seen on the Victoria Line by Tony Bristow and others.

WW2 Pill Box, Bridge Road. (CW)

# Six
# The Auxiliary Fire Service
# 1938-1945

'They did not want to die. Dying meant leaving good friends and happy homes, clear blue skies, the salt of the sea, rounds of golf, walks across the moors, drinks at the club, the wind at night and the scent of log fires. Dying meant they would never know whether or not they had fought in vain.'

Derek Tangye

It was in 1875 that a Public Health Act was formulated to make local authorities provide Fire Hydrants for the fighting of fires. This was not a problem for districts like Croydon with their own water works but the cost involved was too much for at least half the country's local authorities.

Beckenham was one of the richer districts and by 1938 Beckenham's Fire Brigade was considered efficient and modern. This was when the Fire Brigade Act of July 1938 demanded the recruitment of an auxiliary fire service as part of the country's Civil Defence Force. In the event of war the pay would be £3 per week for men and £2 for women.

Although the Auxiliary Fire Service only lasted three years before it was unified nationwide as the NFS (National Fire service), the men served their country during the time of the Luftwaffe's most severe attacks on London in the blitz of 1940/41 and the assault by flying bombs and V2s in 1944/45 when Beckenham was in 'Doodlebug Alley'. They continued until they were disbanded in 1945. Oddly they were always considered civilians and the part timers were voluntary unpaid.

Inside an AFS sub-station (BL)

The main Beckenham fire station in Bromley Rd had five substations, each manned by one regular fire service commanding officer and AFS members. These were sited at

1. The Standard Bank of South Africa ground in Stanhope Grove (now Amida)
2. The Midland Bank ground in Lennard Rd
3. Elmers End bus garage
4. Barclay Perkins sports pavilion between South Eden Park Rd and Wickham Way
5. Burnham's factory in Kangley Bridge Rd.

The West Wickham fire station, only opened in 1939, had a single substation in Coney Hall at Gates Green Rd. Another substation, part of the Penge AFS, was located later in Copers Cope Rd at the Lloyd's Bank sports ground. There were also 36 Action stations in

Firemen practise with the pumps in Kelsey Park. They aimed at targets that spun round when hit. (MC)

private houses where a trailer pump would be stored, often by a taxi driver/part time fireman. Residents would provide nightly accommodation for the crews. Beckenham included ambulances in their service although this was by no means usual. The regular firemen and the auxiliaries worked together with one accord for the success of the service as a whole. Beckenham was part of the outer London area K which included Erith, Crayford, Bexley, Chislehurst and Sidcup, Orpington and Petts Wood, Bromley, Beckenham and Penge. Croydon was in area L, the other southern outer London group.

Alfred Breck, born 1913, lived with his brothers and sister in Eden Rd, Elmers End. He joined the Penge AFS in 1938 as he was in a reserved occupation as an electrician which was useful when the station doors failed. He served through some of the worst incidents like the Churchfields Rd and Elmers End bus garage disasters.

Alfred remembers the war artist, J. Kingsley Sutton, for whom he acted as a steward at an exhibition at the Royal Academy in August 1941 where five of Sutton's paintings were shown. Sutton was a member of the Beckenham AFS at the Midland Bank Sportsground and his paintings were as follows:

Beckenham crew at work on the London wharves in December 1940
Casualty in the Battle of the Flames
Cleaning the morning after the blitz
A London Fire Force Officer
The Man on the Branch.

Living now in Whitstable with one of his daughters, Alfred muses over his time in the AFS and how shabbily they were treated at the end of the war. Being civilians, they were not eligible for demob suits and had to remove the buttons from their uniforms in exchange for cards of safety pins. They walked away in their tired old uniforms held up by safety pins to renew their lives in Civvy Street.

Casualty in the battle of the flames.
Painting by Beckenham AFS member, J Kingsley Sutton (RB)

Graves of the seven AFS men at St John the Baptist, West Wickham. (PM)

March and April 1941 were bad months for Beckenham. Thirty auxiliary firemen were killed in three incidents: first on the 19 March, five men were killed in Plaistow Rd, West Ham; then four men died as a result of a bomb falling in Wickham Rd, Beckenham on 16/17 April; lastly and worst of all, twenty one men died at Old Palace School in Bow 19/20 April.

The five Coney Hall men who were killed on 19 March at Plaistow Rd, West Ham were buried at St John the Baptist West Wickham on 23 March. The procession with the five flower-covered hearses stretched from the top of Corkscrew Hill down the road to the church. Denis Fitzgerald had been bellringer, Sunday school teacher and church council member of St John's. Charles Drew was on duty at the Coney Hall substation two nights out of three. Leslie Palmer's coffin was borne by his four brothers, one an auxiliary fireman and the other three in the Home Guard. Frederick Moore, a coach builder, was the first of the five to join the AFS. Stanley Short, the eldest at 36, left two children.

Four Beckenham men were killed at the junction of Court Downs Rd with Wickham Rd on 16/17 April, three outright, Richard Beacon, David Chalmers and Stanley Hudders and one, Jack Maynard, died seven months later from his injuries. The driver, 29 year old Carl Taylor, was awarded the George Medal for returning to the blazing fire engine to drag out the injured Maynard helped by a Canadian, Gunner Jack Chambers of the Royal Canadian Artillery. The Canadian was also awarded the George Medal in January 1942. Carl Taylor was the owner of the hairdressing business 'Maison Carl' in Beckenham Rd.

An HE bomb had fallen on a house in Wickham Rd and as fragments pierced the petrol tank, the appliance had burst into flames. Twelve year old Peter Grey walked with his father from Elmers End to check that his grandmother at 22 Chancery Lane was all right. He remembers the shattered fire appliance and the goggles and pipe of a fireman's respirator on the road. Why the 280ft Crystal Palace tower had been felled at midday on the 16 April, many thinking that the tower was a navigation aid for the Luftwaffe.

Three victims of the Court Downs Rd incident were buried in area H3 in the Beckenham cemetery. Jack Maynard has a handsome black memorial that is also in memory of his wife Hilda Bertha Esther who died in January 2003. Beside the Maynard grave is that of David James Chalmers and Stanley Richard Hudders, 'Stout Fellas.' 'Taxi' Hudders was a stagehand-carpenter-electrician before the war. Richard 'Ginger' Beacon, handyman and Jack-of-all-trades, was buried at Sittingbourne.

Three days later, 21 Beckenham firemen died at Old Palace School, Leonard St, Poplar, which had been made a sub fire station since the children had all been evacuated. Four crews had been ordered from Woodside, where things had eased, to the old four storey LCC Board School in Bromley by Bow where the situation was getting worse. Arriving at 1.30am on 20 April they were all killed by the landmine that fell on the school at 1.53am. The mine on a parachute penetrated the building and came down the stairs where it exploded killing two women outright. One was only recognised by the piece of blue crochet she was making.

AFS Graves: on left is that of Chalmers & Hudders; on right lie Jack Maynard and his wife Hilda; Jack died as a result of the Court Downs Road bomb in 1941. (PM)

Decorated fire engines used in the Funeral Procession for the 19 Beckenham AFS killed on the night of 19-20 April 1941 at the Old Palace School Poplar. (MC)

Ernest Beadle (left) and his brother-in-law Norman Mountjoy at Norman's marriage to Olive Beadle at Christ Church, Saturday June 15 1940. (OH)

The firemen were killed by the blast and the collapse of the building.

On the 25 April the firemen were buried in a mass grave at the Beckenham cemetery after a memorial service at the parish church of St George by Canon Boyd and a solemn procession through the town. The grave was dug entirely by their comrades and was softened by masses of daffodils. The 19 coffins were placed in St George's church on the Wednesday before the service and guarded by firemen. It took half an hour for the procession to pass any point on the route to the cemetery. After the coffins had been placed in the grave, posies and bunches of flowers were dropped in and there were 350 wreaths.

Two firemen, Norman Mountjoy and Ernest Beadle, the husband and brother of Olive Mountjoy, both killed with the other 19 at Old Palace School in Bow, were buried the previous day beside those at West Wickham. Olive Beadle and Norman Mountjoy had married at Christ Church on Saturday June 15 1940 just ten months before the tragic incident. The memorial stone at the Elmers End cemetery was unveiled seven months later by Mayor Sampson on Saturday 13 December 1941. Among those present with the widows and close relatives were Sir Edward Campbell MP, the Town Clerk Mr C Eric Staddon, Councillors of Beckenham and Kent County and officers from the police and fire service. After a short service by Canon Boyd, trumpeters of the London Fire Brigade sounded the Last Post.

Ken Bowles worked at the stock exchange and was a keen sportsman especially at hockey. He married Mollie in 1938 having met through the marriage of their brother and sister. He joined the AFS at the outbreak of war and when he was killed his son John was just a year old.

When Mollie Bowles was 87 she still remembered her feelings vividly when she heard that Ken had been killed.

AFS man, Ken Bowles, who died at the fire at Old Palace School, Poplar April 19/20 1941. (SM)

> *I think we were all aware of the danger the firemen faced. The bombs fell virtually every night and the men were constantly on duty tackling fires, saving people. Beckenham was directly on the flight path to London and the planes used to fly over all the time. I remember one occasion when Ken came back covered from head to foot with soot. He was a wonderful father. He was obsessed with John, holding him in his arms. He had plans to teach him how to play different sports.*
>
> *It was really terrible. I was at home when I heard about it. Somebody from the council was walking up the path. I was standing at the door and he told me what had happened. I was completely devastated.*
>
> *The community was fantastic. It was very different then. We were all in the war together. I don't think without them I could have coped. It was that and my Christian faith that gave me the strength.'*

After the war there was a tremendous demand for council housing that war-torn Beckenham found difficult to satisfy. By 1959, housing blocks were available for about a quarter of the housing queue. They were named after the casualties in the AFS, the Wardens service and the Heavy Rescue and are built at Newlands Park, Churchfields Rd, Seward Rd, Oakfield Ave, Perth Rd and the Chulsa estate.

By the middle of June 1941 the worst of the blitz was over and there was time for parades at Croydon Rd Recreation ground and in West Wickham and recreational activities.

The firemen also helped the war effort from September 1942 to April 1945. Soldering was the speciality of the firemen of RR3 station in Copers Cope Rd where 175,764 condensers and terminals passed through their hands. Firewoman Trixie Rich from Orpington earned the distinction for being the fastest incendiary parachute stitcher in the London area. The men improvised their own workshops to be on hand for fire calls and put in over 302,368 man-hours assembling equipment like mine detectors and cockpit lamps.

Hawthorndene in Southend Road, Beckenham used by part time firemen from November 1941. (MC)

The Action stations were closed with the advent of the NFS in 1941 and a central station was opened at Hawthorndene in Southend Road backing on to Beckenham Place for part-time firemen of area 37. During quiet times these part time firemen did voluntary work such as the redecoration of the children's ward at the Cottage Hospital led by Leading Firemen Harris, McKibben and Weeks with 60 men. They also gave 100 consecutive days service to make damaged houses habitable.

On arrival of the V-bombs, the part time service was immediately in action putting out fires and attending rescue operations.

On the occasion of their 'Stand-down' in March 1945, there was a picture of the firemen of Hawthorndene across the front page of the Beckenham Journal of 10.3.1945. Their celebration dinner had been held at the Regal Ballroom on Thursday 22 February when 150 men had attended. Guests of Honour were Assistant FFC Leeks, Divisional Officer Gordon Smith, Senior Chief Officer Vernon Jones and Chief Officers Jack Morgan, Jameson, Frewer, Bagg and Warner. They were able to give a cheque for £400 to Beckenham Hospital from excess balance and this went towards naming a bed.

The service did not cease with the 'Stand-down' but remained 'On call.' A parade of 5000 part-timers was held in Hyde Park in March 1945.

The remains of the Poplar school were demolished in 1948 and a new school was built on the site in 1952. William Somerville was a member of the Millborne school sub fire station but he was on leave that night and survived the war. His son Frank, who was born after the war, organised a memorial plaque at the school to be unveiled on Saturday 19 April 1997, exactly 56 years later, dedicated to the 34 who lost their lives in the incident with the greatest loss of life in the history of the Fire Brigade. One of the original firemen who attended the unveiling was Alfred Breck.

Martin Ormes, a fireman at Beckenham Road Fire Station, was there to lay one red rose for each of the 34 dead and to recite the following poem.

## The Fireman's Prayer

When I am called to duty God,
Whenever flames may rage,
Give me the strength to save some life,
Whatever be its age.
Help me embrace a little child
Before it is too late,
Or save an older person from
The horror of that fate.
Enable me to be alert
And hear the weakest shout,
And quickly and efficiently
To put the fire out.
I want to fill my calling
And to give the best in me
To guard my every neighbour
And to protect his property.
If according to your will
I have to lose my life,
Please bless with your protecting hands
My children and my wife.

At the ceremony, Martin realised for the first time that his grandfather, Percy Aitchison, was among the 21 Beckenham firemen who perished.

# Seven
# Making Do from 1942

Of course the men suffered as the womenfolk stole their clothes as well as their coupons. My father's grey flannels were converted into a school skirt that kept me going for two years in the sixth form. We were advised to use a pin-striped light suit to make a tailored dress with the stripes of the yoke and front going in different directions. After all, he wouldn't need his clothes until after the war!

Pat Manning

By the end of July 1941, things had quietened down and there were no more raids on Beckenham for eighteen months.

Children were back at school. The cinemas were open and quite spectacular local events were organised albeit with, understandably, war like themes or fund raising efforts to help buy weapons or naval vessels. One of the most exciting was Warship Week in February 1942 which raised some £500,000 to adopt the destroyer HMS Sikh. Processions in Beckenham and West Wickham consisted of models of the ships Golden Hind, the Victory, HMS Sikh, a pirate frigate, a Viking ship and a 'Heath Robinson' ship all built by Civil Defence personnel. Dances, fairs, demonstrations of unarmed combat and bayonet fighting, naval and military bands, comic football and children's modelling competitions were among the events on the great day.

As the coast of Kent and Sussex was closed to the public, the council devised a 'Holidays at Home' scheme with displays, fairs, picnics and sports days in the parks.

Pat Manning standing on left wearing skirt made from her father's grey flannels 1946 at the Girls County Grammar School. (PM)

38

WARTIME CLOTHES SERVICE
by the Lux News Scout

Skirt for Sister

FROM FATHER'S
OLD FLANNELS

NEVER mind when father's grey flannels get too worn for him to wear. They'll make a most attractive skirt for your small daughter.

First, you'll have to unpick the trousers and remove the pockets and the lining. You will then have four main pieces of cloth. Wash these carefully and iron when nearly dry under a damp cloth.

Make the skirt with six main panels — two wider ones for the front and back, and four narrower ones for the sides. Even avoiding the worn parts there should be plenty of material from the top back part of the trousers

to make the centre panels. The side panels are cut from the lower part of the legs; the V-shaped bodice front and cross-over straps at the back, from the front upper part of the trousers.

A good idea, isn't it? And practical, too, because, of course, the skirt will wash beautifully. Use Lux, if you can. Lux lather is so rich that dirt comes out without rubbing. And it is rubbing, you know, that is mainly responsible for felting and shrinking in woollens.

If you can't get Lux and have to use something else, be sure to rinse extra well. If you don't, specks of undissolved soap are likely to cling to the fabric, causing it to mat and get hard. With Lux, you avoid this danger because Lux dissolves completely in lukewarm water and so it rinses out completely, too.

* * *

Lux is 5d. a packet and takes two coupons.

THIS CLOTHES SERVICE IS
SPONSORED BY
THE LUX WASHABILITY
AND RENOVATION BUREAU

Wartime recycling advert (CW)

There was Rosaire's circus and a week's tour of local parks by the Open Air Theatre. It presented 'Much Ado About Nothing' in June followed by the 'Merchant of Venice' at Percy Jones house, Looe Rocks, at 39 Manor Rd. Victor Thornton was the producer and his 'Shylock' was considered a superb piece of work.

A Civil Defence team played the AFS at cricket at the Foxgrove ground to win the trophy donated by Mayor Sampson. It was won by the firemen, mainly due to their excellent fielding.

Rationing was severe (see the Appendix to see how widespread it had become by 1942) and people had to make the best of things. Recipes using potatoes that we could grow in abundance included potato pastry. Double sugar rations (one pound per person per week instead of half a pound) were issued for two summer weeks to encourage us to make plum jam from the particularly good plum crop. There was a campaign for collecting and drying foxglove leaves that could be used for extracting drugs for treating heart disease. Books for paper salvage were collected as a mile of books; one mile was from the Park Langley garage to Shortlands station and another was a circuit from Kent House station and back via the Girls County School in Lennard Rd.

Families were encouraged to exchange to share or pass on Wellingtons and gym shoes to children in need of replacements. The Council even considered supplying children with gym shoes as mothers were reluctant to use up clothing coupons on them but the idea was turned down as it would cost £400. I had a friend who spent all her school years playing lacrosse in two left boots as that was all that was left in the shop, Frost's in Maple Rd.

Gerald Crease has this to say about his life during the war.

*'I don't ever recall being frightened of the war. I suppose I was too young to understand what was happening. I was born in Beckenham in 1936, the only child of Percy and Betty Crease. My earliest memories are of being in the Beckenham Cottage Hospital with scarlet fever and being laid to sleep on stretchers in the corridors. Then I came home to my grandfather's house, Mertonholme at 30, Wickham Rd. He was James Crease, first Freeman of the Borough of Beckenham.*

*We were lucky that our house was never bombed although nearby houses were hit. For a long time afterwards the bombed houses were a playground for the boys and, as I remember, two girls. As nothing was fenced off or boarded up we would go in and out as we wished, up tottery staircases, across upper floors with walls missing and climb out on to rooftops. All highly dangerous but no one came to any harm. There were friends such as Alan Geen, John Martin, The Baker boys, Roger, Martin and Danny from next door, Gillian Severn and Celia Codd.*

*Our garden was large, well over an acre and stretched from Wickham Rd back to Court Downs Rd where there was a little wicker gate that provided a short cut to the High St. It spread sideways behind the gardens of neighbouring houses. There were fruit bushes and trees. My father grew most of our vegetables and we kept chickens, sometimes as many as two hundred. When they were ready for slaughter, it was done by Sam Lale who had a butcher's shop near the Oakhill Tavern. Opposite the house was George Green's builder's yard where I would go on Saturday morning for sawdust for my rabbits. My father would visit the houses along Wickham Rd with a wheelbarrow to collect waste for the chickens.*

*In 1942, I started at Bromley Road Infant Schools where there was an air raid shelter in the playground which on a recent visit I noticed was still there. At home we had a Morrison shelter, a contraption of angle irons supporting a steel top with sides made of steel mesh. We were supposed to shelter in it during raids and I had to sleep in it although my parents never did. When VE day arrived in May 1945, we went to the street party in Chancery Lane. Food and drink was produced from somewhere and trestle tables were set up outside the pub with the road unofficially closed for the occasion.'*

Jean Bogle's father was a warden in the ARP and one day Jean went to see their Pig Club near Hawes Down School. She wished she hadn't because she had to hold a large handkerchief up to her nose! Then they went to the canteen at the depot where a very large tea lady was pouring out cups of tea from an equally large teapot.

Clothes rationing began in September 1941 when 66 coupons were issued to everyone to last until the end of May 1942, 14 needed for a coat and 5 for a pair of shoes so it was time to make do and mend. Eventually the coupons were reduced to 51. The Board of Trade issued a booklet at 3d a copy full of ideas of how to make clothes last longer, 'turn out and renovate' and 'unpick and knit again.'

The girls could all knit and with one clothing coupon buying only two ounces of wool we had instructions to unpick old knitted garments and to wind the wool round a piece of cardboard before washing it to take out the crinkles. Can you imagine knitting with two ply wool and size 14 needles today because it goes further?

Most of us knitted everywhere, perhaps a benefit of no TV? The most horrible garment that we knitted was a swimming costume that stretched to the ground when wet and I remember knitting lacy cotton stockings impossibly uncomfortable to wear. My father suffered hand knitted woollen socks that could be reheeled when they went into holes. One of the hints was to darn holes in woollies and then to cover the darns with embroidered flowers. We were advised to make things on the big side in case they shrank on washing.

We were told that the clothes moths liked warm dark cupboards. Our houses were so cold for most of the winter because of fuel rationing and long chilly winters that it was a wonder any moths could survive. At least once a month we were to beat and shake out our clothes to rid them of eggs and to iron them with a hot iron especially in the pockets.

We were asked 'When did you last clean your shoe brushes and polishers?' These days we can ask 'When did you last clean your shoes?' Warm the brushes by the fire or brush shoes in the sun to make the polish go further. Keep rubber boots in a cool dark place because the sunlight perishes the rubber. Don't dry wet shoes by the fire as it ruins the leather fibres. Do you remember those toe-pieces and half soles that we could stick on our shoes to stop them wearing down? Incidentally every High St had two or three shoe repairers who were always busy.

What about household linen? Sheets folded sides to middle with an uncomfortable seam down the centre. Leave the crockery to drip dry to save on tea towels. Take your towel with you to the office and the hairdresser and buy a new one only when absolutely necessary.

Poor father had to have the collar and cuffs of his shirts removed and reversed to put the worn parts on the other side and his skin gloves and leather belts could be used to make fancy patches on his daughter's dungarees.

Six years plus was a long time for the wardrobes of girls and boys and they were allowed more clothing coupons if they exceeded certain heights and weights. Dresses were made with large hems that could be let down with Vandyke braid to cover the line of the fold and set with pleats and gathers to allow for increase in girth. Many of us had to make two dresses into one as we grew up. The boys made do with government surplus trousers and jackets in very thick rough serge.

Nightdress made from parachute silk, displayed at 1940's evening in Anerley Library, May 2005. (CW)

Finally, don't forget the parachute silk that became the staple fabric of ladies underwear, a sewing group sharing out the panels among their members and the wedding dresses made from unrationed lace. It was not by chance that Princes Elizabeth's wedding dress in 1947 was made entirely of lace!

Several of our bombed churches were still used by their congregations. In August 1945, a year after St Mary's Church had been destroyed by two flying bombs, the congregation gathered for a service on the bombed site led by the Rev. J F Thornhill. He said, 'We had hoped so much that the church would be spared but all day long the bombs seemed to be dropping shorter and I had a strange kind of presentiment that something was going to happen that night.'

In January that year, Christ Church was shattered by the blast from a V1. However, the indomitable Rev. Guy King held a service in the shell of the building and regular services continued after the Parish Hall was cleared of debris.

Seven months before, St George's had most of its windows blown out and tiles removed by two flying bombs in Albemarle and Church Roads. With rain pouring in everywhere, Churchwarden, Captain Walker, a trained engineer, organised a working party with church members, the Home Guard and the people of Beckenham to clear the rubble and protect the building from the weather. The work was hampered by more bombing incidents but services were resumed on a regular basis from Easter 1945.

On the whole Beckenham and Penge were fortunate that most of the houses were of Victorian or Edwardian origin with gardens ranging from a few feet to a few acres in size. All could be used for "digging for victory" (growing seasonal vegetables providing crops for seven months of the year), fruit bushes and rearing rabbits and chickens, prolific suppliers of almost free rabbit and eggs.

Parks, open spaces and the periphery of sports grounds were taken over for some 2,500 allotments or market gardens. Howard Smith of Beckenham Town FC, remembers the bushes still providing soft fruits for some years after the war. But commons and disused grounds like Crystal Palace Park offered rich pickings of blackberries and rose hips (a valuable source of vitamin C) as well as acorns to feed the pigs.

The acorns augmented the scraps deposited in the pig bins that were positioned in most roads. The bins were emptied daily for use as pig swill.

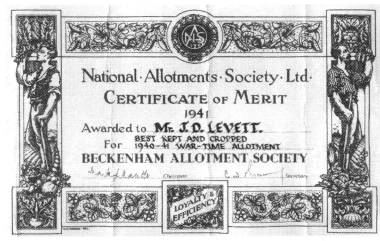

Beckenham Allotment Certificate (ES)

Children found another use for the bins as wickets for cricket played in the the streets.

Exotic foods rarely available these days on offer during the war included frogspawn (aka tapioca pudding), mock suet pudding, bottled vegetables, carrot cookies, banana sandwiches (using turnips flavoured with banana essence), eggless sponge (for those without chickens), "boiled" fruit cake, bubble and squeak, rissoles, oat cakes, slice with a scrape (of whatever one could find), wild shot or reared fresh (rather than Chinese) rabbit and the magnificent Lord Woolton Pie, named after the Minister of Food 1940 - 43. This was compote of boiled potatoes, swedes, cauliflowers and carrots below a crust of potato or wheatmeal pastry, with rabbit added if available.

British Restaurants were established so that the elderly and mothers with young children could enjoy a nourishing meal for a few pence without using their food coupons. Jean Bogle reminds us of the British Restaurant at Elmers End, and David Wood ate with his parents at one in St George's Hall in Beckenham High Street opposite the church.

Patricia Knowlden (who appeared in the 1940's house TV programme) reminisced in the Bromley Borough Local History Newsletter, 'Bromleag' March 2005 of the one in Burnt Ash Lane. On the menu were rabbit pie, steak and kidney or braised liver for 6d a portion. Lentil soup was 1d and sultana roll or rice pudding would fill us up for 2d. A child's meal was 4d, less than 10p today.

Carrot cookies, Spam, Woolton Pie, and other dishes cooked using WW2 recipes. Displayed (and eaten!) in Penge Library, May 2005. (CW)

Patricia has a collection of recipes from her mother-in-law and recommended a variation on the eggless sponge, namely a Golden Cake which uses mixed golden syrup and vinegar instead of egg.

Land Army women were able to bring home extra food on their return from the farms. Mrs Molly Benfield from Penge tells of her time on farms in Otford and on the Kent marshes.

> 'You start a day bending over to pick beans but by the end of the day, you were literally on your knees. I milked the cows. Some farmers treated the women very badly and it was the friendly German and Italian POWs who often helped us complete our day's work.'

Joyce Stanley nee Stonham who married in 1937 and had two little boys, Michael and Gavin, in the early part of the war lived in Forster Rd, while her husband worked for the Admiralty based in Ceylon. He was away for three years but was able to send Joyce one pound of tea per year to eke out her tea ration. He could also send tea to each of his boys and various relations but each could only have one pound. Fortunately he was able to return to his work after the war as a jeweller in Hatton Garden.

Mrs Marian Jones and her husband William were married in 1940 and a year later they moved into a ground floor flat at 81 Thicket Road, Penge. William was an engineer, a reserved occupation, They were not well off, Marian having to give up her job when their first son was born in 1940.

Making do for the Jones meant that furnishing their home relied on second hand and passed down furniture but in 1943 they had saved up to buy some utility furniture, including the sideboard, in the photo (right).

The Jones were not alone in making this sort of purchase. From November 1942 the government had prohibited manufacturers from making any furniture except Utility styles, in order to save raw materials. In the event the sideboard was a very good buy for it remained in use until Mrs Jones died in December, 2004. It can now be seen in the Bromley museum.

Mrs Jones utility sideboard 2005 (CW)

Wartime marriages often had to "make do" when it came to wedding outfits. Helen Oliver (nee Lyford) can trace four members of the Lyford family of Beckenham who were married in the war years. The first was when Alice married Harold Chapman on 1939. The fourth wedding was between Jack and Doris Muff in June, 1944.

Helen's father Jack was in his Home Guard uniform at the wedding of his sister, Clara to Hartley Corlett (also in uniform) in January, 1941. Clara's sister Alice and Jack's fiance Doris Muff were bridesmaids. Their dresses were re-used two years later by the maids at wedding of Eileen Muff and Henry Goodfellow in September, 1943.

People made do when it came to food and clothes but not when it came to the company of family and friends. At that time people shared their lives in a way that we don't now. Help was offered whenever a need was seen. Both the Muff sisters went to the County School in Lennard Road where Doris knew Olive Rippengal.

Above: The marriage of Eileen Muff and Henry Goodfellow, September 1943. St, Francis, West Wickham.
The bridesmaids dresses were those previously used at the wedding in 1941 of Clara Lyford to Hartley Carlett, pictured left. (HO)

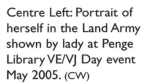

Above: Doris Rushbrook now Pullen, VAD Nurse in the Civil Nursing Reserve Red Cross in the garden of 66 Newlands Park in 1940. (DP)

Right: Another visitor to Penge Library wears her wartime ARP badge with pride, 60 years on. (CW)

Helen Oliver's father Jack Lyford in Home Guard uniform in 1941. (HO)

Jack's sister-in-law, aged 20, Eileen Muff in ATS uniform 27 June 1942. (HO)

# Eight
# The Summer of '44...

'I lay on my mother's bed by her side and, as the engine of the V1 cut out, held my breath, waiting for the explosion. When it came, it was as though the end of the world had come. The house shuddered and the room filled with dust and flying glass; the noise was deafening. It was a warm night on 25 June in 1944 and the time was 9pm. The doodlebug had fallen on the last but one house in a terrace of eight houses diagonally opposite ours. The memories of that night are even after 43 years still vivid and powerful although, like a broken kaleidoscope, they are made up of jagged fragments which no longer fit together in any semblance of order or pattern.'

The composer Carey Blyton

The Beckenham Journal of 16 September 1944 was allowed to publish details of the 11 weeks of summer 1944. Its headline was '71 FLYING BOMBS DROPPED IN BECKENHAM & 20 ON BORDERS with 132 KILLED and 1085 INJURED'. Below are memories of some of the attacks and another in January 1945

## 1944
### JUNE 6TH
The long awaited D-Day landings were welcomed with joy and high expectation
BUT Hitler's revenge weapons or VERGELTUNGSWAFFENS were being built at Pennemunde, a remote island off the Baltic. These were intended to win the war for him

### JUNE 16TH
The first V1's struck on Tootswood and Links Road. Geoffrey Crabb remembers this date well - the day before was his eleventh birthday. He writes that the air raid warning
> 'sounded at 11.30 pm and into the Morrison shelter I went. We were aware of aircraft noise but rather different from usual and when my mother opened the curtains we saw a plane with flames pouring from its rear. My father was outside talking to our neighbour, Jim Tonkin, and he commented on the strange noise of the plane. The raid continued all night but when the All Clear went at 9.30 I emerged from the shelter to get ready for school. Then there was another warning and my mother kept me at home. '

In the early hours of the morning, three ARP wardens were killed at Post 42 in Tootswood Rd and seven of the Heavy Rescue crew who went to the scene were themselves killed at the end of Links Rd by a second flying bomb as they went off duty. Sylvia Muxworthy of the Cator TG told of one of the Heavy Rescue crew who had a narrow escape. This was her father, Gordon Cecil Fred Adcock, who lived in Langley Way and was dropped off on the way home thereby missing the carnage.

### JUNE 25TH
Carey Blyton's story continues as follows.
> 'I was twelve years old. My father, an Air Raid warden, was on duty and my sister was out playing tennis. My first clear memory was of somehow making my way upstairs to the toilet through broken glass, tiles, plaster, household items in bizarre twisted shapes and the acrid smell of cordite. As I sat there with diarrhoea, a reaction to the sudden shock and great fear, I saw the vicar picking his precarious way up the stairs. I said I was very worried about our cat and he went to look for it, crunching over the broken glass.

*I was fascinated by the door of the toilet, no longer on its hinges but halfway down the narrow landing in an insane embrace with the door of my bedroom. I managed to get into the various bedrooms and their mad chaos: the contents of drawers and wardrobes all over, broken mirrors, smashed furniture and plaster, glass and tiles underfoot. In the front bedroom, there were great bulging 'sacks' of shattered window glass held by the mesh, which had stretched but not broken. Frightful splinters of glass as long as kitchen knives were embedded in the wardrobe doors. In my sister's room, the spiral net curtain wires were stretched from one wall to the opposite one. The street was now full of people: air raid wardens, police, ambulance men, firemen, neighbours and my sister, incongruous in her tennis gear.*

*It dawned on me how lucky my mother and I had been. Her worsening rheumatoid arthritis made it impossible for her to go upstairs. We were shocked and bruised but otherwise unharmed. The windows of the conservatory had been sucked outwards into the garden although a glass splinter had severed the flex of my mother's art deco lamp shade, which had fallen on my leg. My father arranged for us to go to my aunt at Eltham and while my mother made her slow progress to the car, I saw the appalling devastation caused by the V1.*

*Someone told me that a lady* (Mrs Annie Florence Dallaway) *had been killed in number 77, where the doodlebug had fallen, but the most amazing sight was a man in a bath in the middle of the road* (it was Mrs Dallaway's son). *Dorothy Jennie Knight from number 82 and John Bowles Adams from number 72a died in hospital the next day*

*A school friend who lived in the house opposite had refused his parents' pleas to come into the Morrison shelter as he went to the window to see where the V1 landed! Since it fell 40 ft in front of his face he was lucky not to have been killed. As it was, he had to have an emergency operation to remove a piece of shrapnel which had pierced his forehead.*

## JUNE 30ND

Mave Preedy (nee Covey) was only four years old that day when she made the trip to the shelter. Her mother had made a rice pudding for lunch that day and Mave sat playing with the nutmeg.

*'The bang of the V1 was terrific. The shelter shook and I could sense my parent's unease. As the all-clear sounded, my father cautiously opened the door. Clouds of dust blew in our eyes and our home was demolished. So was the David Grieg shop of which my father had been the manager. My childish reaction was to bemoan through my dusty tears that I had lost all my dolls and now only had a nutmeg to play with.*

*That lunch time when so many died is indelibly engrained in my memory but the full horror of living through the war years hardly touched me. We thought it fun to sleep downstairs and keep chickens in the back garden, normal to grow our own vegetables. My father was in a reserved occupation so I didn't have an unknown father returning from the war or the horror of one not returning at all. Hearing an air raid siren has no effect on me now but until her dying day my mother would rush to turn off the radio or TV if one sounded. Several years after the war, I saw the war damage list which showed the few shillings my parents received for the loss of our home. Amazingly, our neighbour at number 1 Mackenzie Rd still stands.'*

## JULY 2ND and 28TH.

Rachel Notley describes in the church guide how St George's was very seriously damaged as a result of two flying bombs falling within 200 yards of the building. The first on 2 July was at 7 Albemarle Road at the High Street end when three persons were killed. Three more people died when the second flying bomb fell on houses in Church Road at the St George's Road end. (The aftermath appears on the cover.)

*'The entire roofing was displaced and 35 tons of debris had to be cleared. 38,000 tiles were salvaged and reused with 11,000 new tiles. Led by Captain Walker, recently elected church warden, the band of volunteers enthusiastically set about repairing the damage.*

St, Georges Church (CRN)

*Of the 132 stained glass panels, 111 were destroyed, 14 severely damage, leaving only 7 intact. Rain poured in everywhere and the whole forlorn building rendered quite unusable and even in parts dangerous.'*

## JULY 12TH

Allen Horsley lived over and behind the chemist's and library at the corner of Ravenscroft Rd. He wrote,

*'One early evening, we were all sitting in the garden talking to neighbours, when we saw a V1 travelling towards us. It cut out and we all scattered. When it exploded, my sister and I found ourselves under the stairs. The noise, dust, and sound of bottles crashing inside the chemist's shop were terrifying. Our neighbours had managed to get inside their Anderson shelter but couldn't get out due to the blast distorting the shelter doorway. We were all OK except for the dog and cat. Both had to be put down, the dog suffering from hysteria and the cat with a broken leg.'*

All the houses in Albemarle Road shown in the map were destroyed, plus those in St. Georges and Church Roads and the properties on the east side of the High Street. (CW)

## Around JULY 15TH

Olive Rippengal's sister Doreen, with her daughters Cynthia aged 5, Lesley aged 2 and a friend's baby Peter, waited at Marian Vian to be evacuated. Olive could not leave her sister to manage with three small children plus luggage so instead of going to work she gave the evacuees a hand and found herself holding baby Peter for some hours steadily getting heavier and heavier. By the time they had taken buses to Beckenham Junction station, train to Victoria, waited nearly an hour for the tube to Euston because an earlier train had been bombed, Olive managed to report for work in MI3 in the War Office, keeping notables like Hore Belisha waiting until 4.00pm!

Aftermath of VI entering Elmers End Bus Garage. (LTA)

## JULY 18TH

Tony Johns was employed at Muirheads during the last two years of the war. He writes:

> "The siren had sounded and at the same time, dozens of our bombers were passing overhead. Suddenly above the drone of the bombers we heard the dreaded sound of a doodlebug. It appeared end on through the clouds surrounded by a glare that lit up the stubby wings. We threw ourselves to the ground as it hit the factory opposite and we were blown through the archway of Muirheads uninjured but covered in plaster and brick dust.

That same evening a doodlebug flew in through the open doors of Elmers End Bus Garage. The firewatcher on the roof, John Cunningham, stayed at his post warning of the approaching bomb and was killed outright by the explosion. Sixteen people were killed and thirty-nine were injured. Leonard George, who had served in Heavy Rescue throughout the war, was crushed beneath a wall that fell while he was trying to rescue a man trapped in the garage.

## JULY 22ND

Local historian Doris Pullen's second baby girl was born during a raid earlier in the year so she had two little girls to care for alone while sheltering in the cellar. 'After three days and nights without sleep, luckily I went to stay with an aunt in St Albans when the flying bomb fell in our garden of 66 Newlands Park and made us homeless.'

IN MEMORY OF
JOHN E. CUNNINGHAM
HERBERT W. LEACH
FLORENCE M. RARP
THOMAS W. SHARPE
WALTER J. SINGLEHURST
MICHAEL SMYTHE
CHARLES STARES
FRANK W. STEVENS
FREDK H. WESTBROOM
ALFRED J. WILBOURNE
LONDON TRANSPORT
STAFF
KILLED HERE BY AN
ENEMY FLYING BOMB
18TH JULY 1944

Elmers End Bus Garage staff killed by VI on 18th July, 1944.

66 Newlands Park, home of Doris Pullen. (DP)

The devastation of Beckenham Road after August 2nd, V1 attack. (BL)

As seen from Clockhouse Station. (BL)

At junction of Churchfields Rd. (BL)

Perhaps the young wives with small children and husbands called up in the forces suffered the most during the war Her husband was serving in South Africa and when at last he returned home, everything had changed and they seemed strangers. They divorced in 1952, leaving Doris with three children. Life was never the same for many young couples torn apart by the war.

## AUGUST 2ND

Lunchtime day saw the worst V1 strike when a bomb fell on the restaurant at Clockhouse owned by Mrs Richards killing 26 in the diner and injuring many more as well as demolishing shops and twelve houses with further casualties, making 44 dead in all. They included the grocer, Edwin Fitch, the fishmongers Sidney Hancock and Richard Carpenter and the family of the tailor, Philip Rust. (See also Chapter 9.)

## AUGUST 4TH

Cpl Handel of the Home Guard of 14 Cherry Tree Walk, decided to take a bath in the afternoon but sadly a V1 made a direct hit and he was killed although his wife Ruth and little girl Mary had gone for a walk and both survived. If the name Handel makes you wonder, Jean Bogle, Mary's friend, says he was related to the great composer and that both he and his father from Kingston were called George Frederick Handel.

An appendix summarises where the 71 V1s fell that landed in the eleven weeks of the doodlebug 'blitz.'

## 1945 JANUARY

After a four month lull, more flying bombs, released from Heinkels in the North Sea, struck Britain including the one that fell behind Christ Church on 5 January causing the deaths of 13 people in Lea, Fairfield and Burnhill Rds. Mavis Crawford (nee Leeks), whose father was Assistant Fire Force Commandant Reginald Leeks, was given the following account written by one of the Beckenham firemen.

*'We were all amusing ourselves in the common room of Beckenham fire station with snooker, darts or cards when at about seven o'clock we received the message that a fly-bomb had crossed the coast heading in our direction. The sirens sounded and as they stopped we could hear the bomb approaching. It cut out and there was a deathly hush. A few seconds later it exploded behind us and all the windows and doors were blown in.*

(CW)

(SCC)

*Our 'bells' went down and we were off, driving only 200 yds round the corner to the square containing 30 cottages and a church. The whole lot was flattened. After two hours hard work sending the casualties to the hospital, our Officer-in-Charge received a message that a mother and two small daughters were missing. We found them all in a Morrison shelter which had tipped on its side holding up the roof. The girls were soon out but their mother was a huge woman. We had to enlarge the tunnel. When she arrived at street level she cried, "My corsets, I've left them behind, I must have them." To pacify her, two of us went back in to rescue the corsets but we got out fast as it was all beginning to groan. The whole lot caved in a moment later. We found that the family was that of one of our firemen off duty to visit his mother that evening.'*

# The V2 ROCKETS

Over 5,000 V2s were launched of which a fifth landed on GB. Out of the 517 rockets that fell on London, only five came down in Beckenham. Travelling at four times the speed of sound, a V2 caused a double boom as it broke the sound barrier.

The Midland Bank Sports ground in Lennard Rd received a V2 at 10.50 on 2 January 1945 when the groundsman's wife was seriously injured but survived. A week later Cyphers cricket pitch was hit at 12.15 near the indoor bowling green on 9 January.

On 21 February at 11.21 a V2 fell behind St John's church in the Harvington estate. Fortunately the only fatal casualties were two cows and a chicken although the circle made by the rocket was clearly visible in aerial photographs taken by the RAF in 1946.

On 11/12 March, a V2 fell near Marian Vian School in Shirley Crescent leaving one wing unusable and on 15 March, just after midnight, the final one fell at 73 and 75 Crystal Palace Park Rd causing nine deaths, including the Evening Standard cartoonist, Mr Phillips.

Except for the bomb on Cyphers, the local Press did not report these incidents and the Government said nothing. Officially the V2s did not exist. The only way to trace them was through the obituary columns eg about the fatalities at Crystal Palace Park , or the memories of residents. Among Geoffrey Crabb's 'Brushes with the enemy' is the comment that 'My old school, Marian Vian, was damaged one night by a rocket that fell on the adjoining allotments and our road had a sprinkling of mud and a selection of vegetables.'

The damage caused by the Cyphers V2 was reported at length in the Beckenham Journal in the 13 January issue. It fell on the snow covered cricket pitch with superficial damage to the pavilion. The pre-war winter indoor bowling green, now a store, was badly damaged and the injured were taken to hospital. Mr Marchant the groundsman was fortunately not working at the time but his precious pitch was torn up and covered in rubble. By April the bomb crater had been filled in and cricket captain Rupert Holloway was supervising the repair of the ground. The allotments that had half circled the field were reinstated elsewhere, the pavilion patched up and three hockey pitches were ready for use. This was at the most blitzed sports ground in Beckenham that had received nine assorted bombs and the circle left by the rocket could still be seen years later!

Doris Pullen sums up the impact of the V2 as follows.

> *'I returned home when the V2s started. We could sleep in our beds again. There was less nervous strain with a rocket. If you heard it, it had missed you and you were all right. If it had hit you, you wouldn't have heard it at all and would probably be dead, so what was the use of taking shelter? You couldn't wait all day for a bomb to drop on you so we just carried on as normal.'*

## WHY BECKENHAM & PENGE?

In 1970 Peter Jones joined the Engineering department of the London Borough of Bromley which was housed in the old Beckenham Town Hall. While in the basement looking for some drainage records, he stumbled upon drawings showing the V1 strikes in Beckenham and Penge plotted on 50 inches to the mile Ordnance Survey sheets. He recalled that it was possible to lay a straight edge along the plotted strikes that corresponded to a line through Beckenham to Penge. This resulted in Penge becoming the area the most affected by the flying bombs. Peter doubted that the records survived the move to the Bromley Civic Centre when the use of the Beckenham Town Hall was discontinued.

Penge had a pasting was how the Evening News reporter described his visit to the town after 18 V1's fell in 1944. (VW)

# Nine
# 'Don't come home for dinner'

'That's near where I live,' cried Betty and ran off to use the office telephone. Her home number was down so frantically she tried Else Bates' shop and was relieved when the phone was picked up. 'It's Bet. I can't get Mum on the phone.' It's hit the cookshop,' replied Else. Your Mum's buried but they've spoken to her and they're digging her out now.'

Peter Wiseman

The following piece is a reconstruction based on Peter Wiseman's mother's vivid memories of what was one of the worst tragedies in the South East during the war. She was Betty Wiseman, nee Field, best friend of the late Nancy Tonkin nee Banks co-author with the late Eric Inman of the book 'Beckenham'

The town of Beckenham in Kent, just nine miles from London, had the reputation of being one of the worst-bombed in the south-east during the Second World War. During the 1940/41 blitz, night after night the air was filled with the drone of German bombers as Hitler sought to bring the British to their knees but this story is about the much vaunted Vengeance weapon, the V1 or doodlebug of 1944.

It had been a quiet night on 1 August 1944 and Beckenham's residents woke to another gloriously sunny day. In the garden of 1, Churchfields Rd, Lil Field climbed out of the Anderson shelter with her daughter, Betty and younger son, George. With her were Else Bates, who ran the grocer's shop on the opposite corner of the road and Betty's friend, Blondie.

The shelter was the Fields' pride and joy. It was built in a hole in the ground and was the deepest in the street. Erected by Betty's father, Sid, who ran the family's removal business and brother Bill, it had concrete sides and floor and was entered by steps. A sump hole in the floor drained any moisture and it was always dry. The roof was corrugated iron covered with earth in which the family grew marigolds collected for the manufacture of a drug. The entrance was sealed by a door made from railway sleepers. Piles of sandbags completed a formidable hideaway.

For a year now, this shelter had been the family bedroom since their home had been badly damaged during an air raid. It had been the rear half of the building which housed Les Holyoake's shoe repair shop. The upper storey had been the living room and three bedrooms, while the lower had housed the scullery and outside toilet. Now the walls were all that remained. Betty's father was a warden and spent most nights at the post in Thayers Farm Rd. Bill preferred to sleep in the ruined house or on a camp bed in the garage at the bottom of the garden. It was lined with blankets and sheets which could be sprayed with water in the event of a gas attack.

This was where the Field family returned to each night when the Beckenham Conservative Club closed. But now it was 6.30 in the morning and time to start another day. Betty began to get herself ready for work at the Dowsing factories in Southend Rd by Beckenham Place Park. Hers was part of the war effort and involved making flying suits for the high altitude Flying Fortress based at Hatfield. She also fitted the electrically heated linings to boots and gloves as well as making gun and camera muffs that prevented instruments freezing. George worked in the fruit and vegetable buying department at Poupart's in Covent Garden and, of course, Else Bates had to open her shop.

Lil's husband had a removal job that day and was taking Bill, who had just had a course of injections prior to going abroad driving ambulances for the Red Cross. Else's husband Phil was going along for the ride. He had been a fine footballer in his day playing for the Crystal Palace during the 1920s. Lil was to be on her own but had things to do.

George, Bill and Betty Field in 1939. (PW)

The copper was already bubbling away merrily in the corner of the garden.

'Don't come home for dinner today.' Betty was about to leave as her mother spoke. 'Have something at work as I'm going to wash the bedding from the shelter.'

Betty climbed on her bike and headed for Gray's, the baker on the corner of Thayers Farm Rd. With a pillowcase full of rolls and buns (thirteen for a shilling) for the works canteen, her journey took her past the service entrance for the small shops.

Sherlock the grocer could often be seen sitting with scales outside his house selling windfalls from his apple tree. She went past Jordan's the hairdresser, Wyman's the newsagents, Bill Trendall's café where Betty's family would often enjoy stew and dumplings or bangers and mash, and the Prince Arthur pub.

Betty stopped at 21 Southend Rd at the works canteen before reporting for work at number 31. She clocked in, mindful of the fact that if late she would be fined, the money going to charity. Mrs Moire, the cutter, had a grown up family as did another colleague, Gertie. Betty joined her colleagues in the workshop, mostly 18-year olds like herself and all good friends. Thelma Schwartz, a kapok quilter, Lois and Rose were all Betty's age and they used to travel to London together to the theatre. Their banter was invariably about boys and where they were dancing the previous night.

Betty enjoyed a full social life. Her brother took her dancing every night except Sunday with the normal venues at the Royston ballroom, Regal cinema or the West Beckenham Club. Glenn Miller and his Orchestra ruled the air waves and the dance craze was the jitterbug. Betty also had a boyfriend, Else Bates' son Chuck but he was in the army based in Germany.

Tea break was taken at the bench at 10 o'clock and the girls were glad of a rest having been working since eight. The pay was piece work, sixpence for each dozen plugs attached to heating elements. Betty's best week earned £9.

Lunch time arrived and the girls decided to eat their rolls on the fire escape. Suddenly their reverie was broken by the awful wailing of the air raid siren. The group spotted the barrage balloon go up in Cator Park as they were doing in parks all over the borough.

Then they heard it, the unmistakeable sound of a V1 with its engine that of a badly-tuned motor cycle!

Then they saw it, the familiar shape, greyish in colour and resembling a cross as it clattered into view with flames spitting from its tail.

Betty watched in horror as the flying bomb began to make its way in the general direction of the town. Suddenly the engine cut out and the plane dipped down towards the Regal cinema. Seconds later, an ear splitting explosion rent the air and clouds of smoke belched skywards.

'That's near where I live,' cried Betty and ran off to use the office telephone. Her home number was down so frantically she tried Else Bates' shop and was relieved when the phone was picked up. 'It's Bet. I can't get Mum on the phone.' It's hit the cookshop,' replied Else. Your Mum's buried but they've spoken to her and they're digging her out now.'

Reaching the Regal cinema, Betty found the police were stopping everything so she approached the nearest officer with 'My mother's buried but they're digging her out now.' The policeman asked where she lived and told her she would only get as far as Clockhouse station. Then it would be up to the wardens for further guidance. Once more Betty climbed on to her bicycle, heartened by the news that her mother was alive but frightened as to what state she might be in. Eventually she managed to get as far as Sidney Rd where her gaze took in the tragic scene. Where only that morning had stood a row of shops was now but a row of smoking rubble. The row of houses opposite the shops had gone and the air was filled with the stench of smoke and burning. At least five separate fires were burning fiercely as the many wardens searched for bodies and survivors.

Betty took stock of the situation and reasoned that the wardens would probably stop her if she asked for information so, parking her bicycle against a police box, she avoided the wardens and scrambled over the rubble. An apple tree, still with its apples, stood forlornly among the debris as Betty finally reached where her home used to be.

Men were lifting beams looking for bodies but there stood Lil Field shaken but unharmed. She was blackened by the smoke and two large tear stains streaked her face. The two women just hugged each other and cried.

As Betty and her mother began to come to terms with the enormity of the tragedy, the news concerning it was shocking. The café was full, being lunchtime, and the V1 had landed in the doorway. A survivor who had been in Gray's the bakers told in a tremulous voice how he had seen the missile stand on its nose for a split second before exploding. All the diners were killed instantly with many of the people in the houses and shops, a reported total of 44.

Lil Field (PW)

Another lucky survivor was Arthur Frazer, a swimming friend of Betty's. He had been cycling over the railway bridge when the bomb exploded. Diving for cover, he later found out that his trousers had been blown off in the blast. (He can still be seen at the cricket in Foxgrove Rd and was a keen member of the Beckenham Swimming Club and water polo section.)

Sid and Bill returned later that afternoon but could only get as far as Mackenzie Rd on the other side of the scene. Bill immediately joined the growing band of volunteers searching for survivors and was to continue throughout the night. After a phone call young George returned home. He seemed more concerned with the welfare of his pets than the devastation before him. Toby the dog and the rabbits had been well protected and were unharmed. One duck was found wedged inside a chimney with its wings pinned back, totally unhurt, while one poor chicken had lost all its feathers!

The West Beckenham Club invited them all to come for food and a wash. The steward had a relative living near Hertford North station (famous for the opening sequence of the film 'Oh Mr Porter') and it was to here that Lil, George and Betty set off that evening. This was to be their home for the rest of the war. As a guest house it was also home to twenty GIs and airmen in the basement. Billy was the only GI that Sid would allow Betty to go out with and he drove George and Betty to the station every morning to catch the London train. As they were non-army personnel, they had to lie flat on the floor of the jeep. From here, Betty made the gruelling return trip to Beckenham Junction and all her friends at Dowsing's for the princely sum of 6s 9d.

# Ten
# Standing Down on the Home Front and Victory Celebrations

Residents of the upper end of Clockhouse Rd held their party in the garden behind the William IV which was decorated with flags and bunting. A huge Victory cake had been made for the 50 children after their strawberries and plenty of ice cream.

Beckenham Journal

We began stand down from late 1944 anticipating the end of the war when the V weapons tailed off. A final farewell parade of the Anerley Home Guard Rocket Anti-Aircraft Battery was held on 3 December 1944. A ceremonial march ended up with addresses at the Odeon Cinema, Penge. The official stand down of the country's part-time AFS was held in Hyde Park by 5,000 part-timers in March 1945 although the service remained 'On Call.'

The WVS celebrated its stand-down in the lovely garden of Robert Young in Oakwood Ave but was asked to 'Stand-To' for the next two years as so much remained to be done. The WVS was a back up service of women willing to do anything to help, from sewing and knitting to first aid, home nursing, canteens and clearing up the broken glass after a raid. Women always described themselves as 'housewives' and so the 'Housewives Service' of the WVS was formed. A member displayed a Housewives Service card in the window.

Ernest Gowers inspects the firemen at 'Stand down' in Hyde Park with Assistant Fire Force Commander, Reg Leeks, looking on. (MC)

Mrs Hudson was one such woman. There will never be a marble statue erected nor will she have everlasting fame even though, after loyal and unceasing service to the WVS, she met her death in the great May raids in 1941. She was in her Anderson shelter when a direct hit blotted out the little family of Mr and Mrs Hudson with their son.

Wardens were having their final meetings all over the borough but West Wickham's posts 55 and 56 organised a Great Victory Party at Hawes Down in August 1945 before bowing out.

The removal of 150 street shelters, wardens posts and EWS (emergency water supply static water tanks) was one of the first concerns of the council. Dr Edden asked for permission to stand down the Mobility Service that he had run throughout the emergency to provide immediate medical help for casualties. The army helped with the clearing up but you can still see some of the old brick buildings about the borough and the surface shelters recalled by Gerald Crease remain in the playground of Bromley Road Infant School to this day.

This plaque is in memory of all the ARP wardens who died in WW2. It is by St. Mark's school on the site of ARP post 40. (PM)

55

Mobile medical team 1943-45, led by Dr Edden (2nd from left in 2nd row). (FB)

Bone bins attached to lamp posts for residents to deposit waste bones were left for a while. We had not realised the salvage value of bones and threw away three quarters of them but they were 100% useful to the war effort. The bones that were imported to replace those thrown away were equivalent to the carrying capacity of one merchant ship each month.

Three thousand tons of bones supplied 300 tons of grease for making explosives, soap and for lubrication, 450 tons of glue for paints and electrical goods and enough bonemeal to fertilise 108,000 tons of potatoes.

Plotholders with allotments all over the borough were being given notice to leave. Those using the Beckenham Football Club ground were asked to quit and the owner of the demolished house at number 25 Broomfield Rd asked for his garden to be derequisitioned as he wanted to cultivate it himself! Craters on allotments were being filled in but the top soil was buried leaving sticky clay on top.

The Beckenham Emergency Committee announced their raid figures as follows:

| | |
|---|---:|
| Alerts | 1,201 |
| Enemy incidents | 1,500 |
| Defence incidents | 185 |
| HE & UX bombs | 973 |
| Parachute mines including 2 UX | 13 |
| Incendiaries, phosphorus and oil bombs | about 10,000 |
| Fatalities | 351 |
| Seriously injured | 602 |
| Slightly injured | 1,151 |

UX=unexploded

Beckenham Civil Defence

**Disbandment Dinner Party**

of

Emergency Committee Members and Chief Officers

(The " Parlour Boys ")

MEMENTO MENU CARD

October 20th, 1945.

The General Election was held on 5 July 1945 but by the time the results were announced on 26 July, our elected MP Sir Edward Campbell had died. The by-election was won in November by Harold Macmillan who had lost his seat at Stockton at the General Election.

Macmillan's campaign had been strongly supported by Winston Churchill who accompanied him on a drive through the constituency from Anerley Hill, Maple Rd, Penge High St, Beckenham Rd, Beckenham High St, Beckenham Lane, Bromley High St, Mason's Hill and Bromley Common on 10th November. The calvacade was interrupted near Clock House Station by Bill Field who presented Winston Churchill with a captured German sword. Peter Wiseman tells how Bill had driven Red Cross ambulances for the army to transport survivors from the German concentration camps. He had driven into Belsen shortly after the camp was liberated in April 1945 and came home with the sword and uniform of the notorious camp commandant Josef Kramer. The sword is kept in the archives at Chartwell.

Bill Field with his Red Cross ambulance in Germany (left) and the sword (above) that he took from the camp commandent of Belsen.
(PW & PM)

In November, 1945 he stopped a by-election calvacade by Sidney Road Beckenham to present the captured German sword to Winston Churchill in Macmillan's car.
(CW)

VE day fancy dress party in Aviemore Way. Janet Lambert is the central shepherdess and on her left, the shepherdess with a bouquet is actually a boy, Tony Booth. (JL)

For many of us, the end of the war in Europe is remembered by the VE (Victory in Europe) day parade in The Mall. Frances Weiss junior was a patrol leader in the Boy Scouts and acted as a steward. What most impressed him were two Greek soldiers at the front of the parade in white kilts and with great pom poms on their shoes. Frances walked behind 10 Downing St and saw Winston returning from the Palace being slapped on the back and congratulated by everyone he passed.

Francis Weiss's brother, Neils, was a prisoner of war but when he returned, being fluent in German, he was transferred to Intelligence and sent back to the same camp as Commandant!

The children enjoyed their street parties throughout the borough and the adults just rejoiced that the lights could go on again and that the raids had really finished at last. Whit Monday saw the Mayor, Mayoress and Cllr Mrs Frost as the guests of the 150 children in Aviemore Way. The visitors sat on a stage built from Morrison shelters where Bill Sweet, dressed as an overgrown schoolboy, kept the party amused with his jokes throughout the afternoon. After tea of blancmange, iced cakes, cherries, trifles and pineapple, a ventriloquist, a conjuror and a cartoonist kept the party going for an hour. Then they all went home because it RAINED, to continue their celebrations the following Saturday!

Finish of the wheel-barrow race at Croydon Road Rec. (CW)

Residents of the upper end of Clockhouse Rd held their party in the garden behind the William IV which was decorated with flags and bunting. A huge Victory cake had been made for the 50 children after their strawberries and plenty of ice cream. They were all given sweets and biscuits while they had races at which everyone had a prize of savings stamps. The manager of the Elmers End Odeon had provided a microphone for a talent competition and there was also a Punch and Judy show. Shortly after dark, they had a bonfire with fireworks to the delight of the children and dancing to piano and accordion.

VJ (Victory in Japan) Day was celebrated in Beckenham with a two-day programme of sports, concerts, dancing, floodlighting and bonfires all arranged almost overnight. Reading about this sixty years on, it is striking how the Wardens' Service, AFS and local people stepped in to organise the proceedings on the spot. Reg Leeks of the AFS and Warden C Burt set out the course in Croydon Rd Recreation ground for fun races like potato, sack, wheelbarrow, 3-legged, obstacle cycle, egg and spoon, thread the needle, slow cycle and under fives. The war-time concert party 'The four of us' (Ida Pool, Violet Graham-Williams, Vernon Jones and Victor Thornton) amused a crowd of 2,000 for over two hours who then danced to the music of Fotheringham's Dance Band.

The Rt Hon Winston Churchill replies to the Mayor on the occasion of his award of Freeman of Beckenham at Chartwell. (SC)

Coney Hall's Victory Queen was Joan Wallace and VJ + one day saw professional entertainers like the conjuror Harold Beaumont amusing the children in Blake's Park. At the same time we could always go to see Elizabeth Taylor and Mickey Rooney in 'National Velvet' at the Regal.

Perhaps the most notable decision made by the Beckenham Council was to invite the Rt Hon Winston Leonard Spencer Churchill to become a Freeman of the Borough in a ceremony that took place at Chartwell on Monday 28 October 1946. Among the words spoken when the resolution was passed to honour the Rt Hon Mr Churchill MP were these:

> 'When the danger was greatest and there seemed little if any ground for hope that
> we could possibly survive the ordeal, then it was that Mr Churchill constantly rallied and
> supported us and the rest of the nation by his words and strength of purpose.'

The scroll was designed by Mr Sindall a wartime Civil Defence Staff Officer and sealed in a bronze casket made by the Beckenham foundry, Butler-Jones (nameplates) Ltd to the design of Mr Robin Day and Mr Yabsley of the Beckenham Art School. The delegation of the Beckenham Council, which was introduced by the Rt Hon Harold MacMillan MP for Bromley, included the present and three past Mayors. In his speech acknowledging the honour, Mr Churchill said

> 'Beckenham is not far from my home in the heart of beautiful Kent. It stands in the well
> known track of "Bomb Alley" and I fear that many marks of those ordeals still remain
> among you.'

The bronze casket is now on view at the War Cabinet rooms in Westminster.

(PW2)

Sixty years on at the house of Pat and John Williams, there was a VE Day party over two days on the 7 and 8 May 2005 to celebrate just being alive. The guests brought their own tea including spam and egg sandwiches that they put on long tables and shared with each other. Many came dressed for VE Day, including war veterans in uniform. They sang wartime songs and Pat put on a drama including Winston Churchill's wartime speeches. The weather behaved itself and a good time was had by all.

Like this book, the party was in appreciation of all those who worked and lost their lives so that we and our families are able to enjoy our lives today.

We learnt from the war. In terms of new opportunities and experiences, it left us determined at its end to make more of our lives and to build a new world for the survivors and their children.

Hazel Cummings enjoys her holiday at Swanage after the war. (JB2)

The information in the Appendices represents the best known to the authors at this time.

# Housing blocks named after firemen killed

| Surname of fireman | No | and incident | Site of housing block |
|---|---|---|---|
| Aitchison | 1 | Old Palace School, Poplar | Churchfields Road, BR3 |
| Bailey | 2 | Old Palace School, Poplar | Bailey Place, SE 26 |
| Barber | 3 | Old Palace School, Poplar | Westbourne Rd, SE26 |
| Beacon | 4 | Court Downs Road, Beckenham | Border Crescent SE26 |
| Beadle | 5 | Old Palace School, Poplar | Westbourne Rd, SE26 |
| Bowles | 6 | Old Palace School, Poplar | Westbourne Rd, SE26 |
| Carden | 7 | Old Palace School, Poplar | Newlands Park, SE26 |
| Chalmers | 8 | Court Downs Road, Beckenham | Border Crescent, SE26 |
| Deans | 9 | Old Palace School, Poplar | Newlands Park, SE26 |
| Drew | 10 | Plaistow Rd, West Ham | Oakwood Ave, BR3 |
| Endean | 11 | Old Palace School, Poplar | Seward Rd, BR3 |
| Farley | 12 | Old Palace School, Poplar | Seward Rd, BR3 |
| Fitzgerald | 13 | Plaistow Rd, West Ham | Oakwood Ave, BR3 |
| Hall | 14 | Old Palace School, Poplar | Bailey Place, SE26 |
| Healey | 15 | Old Palace School, Poplar | Bailey Place, SE26 |
| Hudders | 16 | Court Downs Road, Beckenham | Churchfields Road, BR3 |
| Kite | 17 | Old Palace School, Poplar | Bailey Place, SE26 |
| Maynard | 18 | Court Downs Road, Beckenham | Churchfields Road |
| Minter | 19 | Old Palace School, Poplar | Bailey Place, SE26 |
| Moore | 20 | Plaistow Rd, West Ham | Oakwood Ave, BR3 |
| Mountjoy | 21 | Old Palace School, Poplar | Bailey Place, SE26 |
| Palmer | 22 | Plaistow Rd, West Ham | Perth Rd, BR3 |
| Parcell | 23 | Old Palace School, Poplar | Newlands Park, SE26 |
| Parfett | 24 | Old Palace School, Poplar | Seward Rd, BR3 |
| Plant | 25 | Old Palace School, Poplar | Newlands Park, SE26 |
| Roots | 26 | Old Palace School, Poplar | Seward Rd, BR3 |
| Short | 27 | Plaistow Rd, West Ham | Perth Rd, BR3 |
| Vick | 28 | Old Palace School, Poplar | Lennard Rd, SE26 |
| Woodland | 29 | Old Palace School, Poplar | Lennard Rd, SE26 |
| Wotton | 30 | Old Palace School, Poplar | Lennard Rd, SE26 |

# Their homes and next of kin

| Surname | Forenames | Age | Kin | Address |
|---------|-----------|-----|-----|---------|
| Aitchison | Percy Charles | 27 | Robert & Eugenie Aitchison (parents) | 20 Copse Ave, W W |
| Bailey | Ronald Mark | 25 | Stella Irene Lilian (wife) | 194 Albert Rd, S Norwood |
| Barber | Alan Charles | 26 | Winifred Rose (wife) | 6 Fairford Close, Shirley |
| Beacon | Richard | 27 | Mr & Mrs R Beacon (parents) | Maidstone Rd, Borough Gr |
| Beadle | Ernest Reginald | 32 | Florence M (wife) | 211 Birkbeck Rd |
| Bowles | Kenneth John | 30 | Mollie (wife) | 27 Beckenham Rd, W W. |
| Carden | Harry John | 29 | Amy Amelia (wife) | 7 Mounthurst Rd, Hayes |
| Chalmers | David James | 31 | Mr & Mrs Ernest William (parents) | 10 Maberley Rd, |
| Deans | Robert Johns | 28 | Mrs E L Deans (mother) | 144 The Grove, W W |
| Drew | Charles Wesley Messenger | 27 | W.M. Drew (wife) | 38 Keswick Rd, W W |
| Endean | Frank James | 36 | Daisy Ellen (wife) | 34 Aviemore Way |
| Farley | Cecil | 43 | E F M Farley (wife) | 5 Linden Leas, W W |
| Fitzgerald | Denis Gerald | 28 | Gwendolene (wife) | 30 Keswick Rd |
| Hall | George John Joseph | 30 | Ethel Beatrice (wife) | 44 Warwick Rd, Anerley |
| Healey | Leslie Thomas | 32 | Aimee Mary (wife) | 15 Greenview Ave, Shirley |
| Hudders | Stanley Richard | 30 | Lilian May (wife) | 14 Pelham Rd |
| Kite | Albert Victor | 36 | Gertrude (wife) | 166 Village Way |
| Maynard | John Henry | 37 | Hilda Bertha Esther (wife) | 21 Gowland Rd |
| Minter | Alfred Edward | 46 | Anne (wife) | 48 Aylesford Ave |
| Moore | Frederick Walter | 35 | Kenelm & Alice (parents) | 22 Lawrence Ave, Carshalton |
| Mountjoy | Norman Richard Charles | 30 | Olive (wife) | 11 Ash Grove W W |
| Palmer | Leslie John | 31 | Doris Maude (wife) | 16 Lawrence Rd, W W |
| Parcell | Frederick George | 32 | Maud (wife) | 28 Love Lane, S Norwood |
| Parfett | Martin Charles | 31 | Nellie Ethel (wife) | 296 Pickhurst Rise, W W |
| Plant | William Charles | 26 | Matilda L (wife) | 22 Sultan St |
| Roots | Leonard | 31 | E S Roots (wife) | 10 Avenue Rd, Anerley |
| Short | Stanley | 36 | Florence Lilian(wife) | 94 Addington Rd, W W |
| Vick | Edgar William | 38 | | 234 Eden Way |
| Woodland | Walter John | 41 | Doris Sylvia (wife) | 68 Links Way |
| Wootton | Herbert Charles | 30 | Irene Dorothy (wife) | 78 Upper Elmers End Rd |

The details shown in the above table are provided by the Commonwealth War Graves Commission on the internet www.cwgc.org

## Houses of the Chulsa Estate named after Civil Defence casualties WWII

| Name | Date of death | Site of incident | Next of kin & address |
|---|---|---|---|
| Ernest Stanley **Agate** HR | 16.6.1944 | Links Rd West Wickham | Ruth Agate (wife ) 70 Wiverton Rd, Sydenham |
| Henry John **Bailey** HR | 16.6.1944 | Links Rd West Wickham | S M Bailey 2 Shirley Crescent, Elmers End |
| Richard **Beacon** AFS | 17.4.1941 | Court Downs/ Wickham Rd junction | Mr & Mrs R Beacon (parents) Rayleigh, Maidstone Rd, Borough Green |
| Harold Albert **Browne** HR | 16.6.1944 | Links Rd West Wickham | Muriel Alice Lydia Browne (wife) 139 The Avenue, West Wickham |
| David James **Chalmers** AFS | 17.4.1941 | Court Downs/ Wickham Rd junction | Mr & Mrs E W Chalmers (parents) 10 Maberley Rd, |
| Frank William **Burton** HR | 16.6.1944 | Links Rd West Wickham | May Burton (wife) 136 Kingsway, |
| Gladys Muriel Blinkhorn-**Hay** ARP | 4.12.1940 | Wardens' Post 40 Queen Anne Ave | F W Blinkhorn-Hay (husband) 6 Park Hill Rd, |
| Leonard **George** HR | 18.7.1944 | Elmers End bus garage | Jessie Ellen George (wife) 17 Worbeck Rd, Anerley |
| Leslie Frederick **Hurst** ARP | 4.12.1940 | Wardens' Post 40 Queen Anne Ave | A L Hurst wife 89 Queen Anne Ave, |
| Lawrence Walter **Lathwood** HR | 16.6.1944 | Links Rd West Wickham | Nita Muriel Lathwood (wife) 51 Rose Walk, |
| Florence and Reginald **Seath** ARP | 16.6.1944 | Wardens' Post 42 Tootswood Rd | Mr & Mrs Henham (parents) Mrs Seath (mother) Courtlands Lodge, Hayes Lane. Originally from Faversham |
| Adolphus George **Ripley** ARP | 16.6.1944 | Wardens' Post 42 Tootswood Rd | Mrs A G Ripley (mother) 18 Tootswood Rd, |
| George Victor **Wingham** MM HR | 16.6.1944 | Links Rd West Wickham | Mr & Mrs James Wingham (parents) 121 Stanhope Grove, |

ARP - Air Raid Precautions (Wardens' Service)
HR - Heavy Rescue
AFS - Auxiliary Fire Service

### The Chulsa Estate

Walter Carter was a partner in Cresswell & Co who owned the Chulsa Tea Estates in the Dooars in the foothills of the Himalayas. When Walter retired he bought a large house on Sydenham Hill that he called Chulsa where his four daughters and three sons were brought up. Sadly, after the family left in 1930, the house was burned to the ground and the site lay derelict. Then in 1953 it was planned to develop it into Beckenham's largest housing estate with one of the roads called Chulsa Rd and the other Border Crescent. The Penge tunnel passed beneath.

The name Border Crescent dates from 1870 when it was on the border between Penge and Lewisham. This has led to problems because it has become a political no-man's land between the Bromley and Lewisham Boroughs with rent and rates paid by some to Bromley and others to Lewisham. The children's schooling is split between the two boroughs also the voting in the elections.

## A-Z List of roads bombed in Beckenham during the blitz

| Where | Date |
|---|---|
| Abbots Way | 20.1 43 |
| Abbots Way | 6/7.9.40 |
| Abbotsbury Road WW | 28/29.10.40 |
| Abbotsbury Road WW | 18.10.43 |
| Addington Road WW | 1/2.11.40 |
| Addington Road WW | 11/12.10.40 |
| Addington Road WW | 7.10.40 night |
| Addington Road WW | 16/17.4.1941 |
| Albemarle Road (2) | 7.10.40 night |
| Albemarle Road (5) | 16/17.4.41 |
| Ancaster Rd | 14.9.40 pm - 16.9.40 |
| Ancaster Rd | 19.1.41 |
| Arrol Rd | 14.9.40 pm - 16.9.40 |
| Ash Tree Close WW | 14.3.1944 |
| Ashleigh Rd | 1/2.10.40 |
| Balmoral Avenue | 7/8.11.40 |
| Balmoral Avenue | 10.3.41 |
| Barnfield Wood Rd | 12.9.40 night |
| Barnfield Wood Rd | 14.9.40 pm - 16.9.40 |
| Barnfield Wood Rd | 13/14.10.40 |
| Barnfield Wood Rd | 18.10.43 |
| Barnfield Wood Rd | 19/20.10.40 |
| Barnfield Wood Rd (2) | 16/17.4.41 |
| Barnmead Road (2) | 16/17.4.41 |
| Beckenham Baths | 12.1.41 |
| Beckenham Cricket Club | 18.11.40 |
| Beckenham Place Golf Course | 23/24.11.40 |
| Beckenham PO | 8.11.40 |
| Beckenham RFU | 7/8.11.40 |
| Beckenham Road near Baths | 20.1.1943 |
| Beckenham Road | 14.9.40 pm - 16.9.40 |
| Beckenham Road | 7/8.11.40 |
| Beckenham Road | 29.11.40 |
| Beckenham Road | 20/21.10.40 |
| Belmont Rd | 22/23.9.40 |
| Bevington Rd | 17/18.9.40 night |
| Birchtree Ave WW | 16/17 4 1941 |
| Birkbeck Rd | 20/21.10.40 |
| Blakeney Rd | 3.10.40 am |
| Blandford Rd | 7/8.11.40 |
| Blandford Rd | 16/17.4.41 |
| Bolderwood Way WW | 21/22.10.40 |
| Bolderwood Way WW | 1/2.11.40 |
| Bourne Way WW | 6/7.9.40 |
| Bourne Way WW | 16/17 4 1941 |
| Bourne Way WW | 1/2.11.40 |
| Brabourne Rise | 21/22.10.40 |
| Brabourne Rise | 6.11.40 |
| Brabourne Rise | 3.10.40 am |
| Brackley Rd | 16/17.4.41 |
| Brackley Rd | 3.10.40 am |
| Brackley Rd | 14.9.40 pm - 16.9.40 |
| Brackley Rd | 15.11.40 |
| Brackley Rd (2) St Paul's Church | 12.9.40 night |
| Brackley Rd/Southend | 2.11.40 |

| Where | Date |
|---|---|
| Braemar Gardens WW | 10.5.41 |
| Braeside | 11/12.10.40 |
| Bramerton Rd | 18/19.9.40 night |
| Broadoaks Way | 6/7.9.40 |
| Bromley Gardens | 29.11.40 |
| Bromley Gardens | 7.10.43 |
| Bromley Rd | 7.10.40 night |
| Bromley Rd | 16/17.4.41 |
| Broomfield Road | 5.1.41 |
| Broomfield Road | 10.3.41 |
| Broomfield Road, nos 21 to 27 | 19/20.10.40 |
| Burnhill Road | 12.1.41 |
| Bushey Way | 6.11.40 |
| Bushey Way | 6.11.40 |
| Bushey Way | 13/14.10.40 |
| Bushey Way | 16/17.4.41 |
| Byne Road | 27.12.40 |
| Cator Park | 17.10.40 |
| Cator Park | 16/17.10.40 |
| Cator Road | 17.10.40 |
| Cator Road | 11.1.41 |
| Cator Road | 1/2.11.40 |
| Cator Road, Ibis Sports Ground | 29.12.40 |
| Cator Rd/Lennard Rd (kindergarden) | 29.12.40 |
| Cedars Road | 5.6.43 |
| Cedars Road | 16/17.4.41 |
| Cedars Road | 22/23.9.40 |
| Cedars Road | 14.9.40 pm - 16.9.40 |
| Celtic Avenue | 7.10.43 |
| Charleville Circus | 15.3.41 |
| Cherry Tree Walk WW | 20.3.41 |
| Cherry Tree Walk WW | 14.9.40 pm - 16.9.40 |
| Cherry Tree Walk WW | 16/17.4.41 |
| Chestnut Ave (2) WW | 16/17.4.41 |
| Churchfields Rd | 16/17.4.41 |
| Clockhouse Road | 7/8.11.40 |
| Clockhouse Road | 9/10.10.40 |
| Clockhouse Road | 14.9.40 pm - 16.9.40 |
| Clockhouse Road | 11.9.40 |
| Clockhouse/Hampden Road corner | 30.8.40 |
| Coney Hall WW | 23/24.10.40 |
| Coney Hall Recreation Ground WW | 16/17.4.41 |
| Coney Hall Recreation Ground WW | 6/7.9.40 |
| Coney Hall Recreation Ground WW | 1/2.11.40 |
| Coney Hill Rd WW | 16/17.4.41 |
| Cooks Sports Ground | 29.11.40 |
| Copers Cope Road | 28/29.9.40 |
| Copers Cope Road | 9/10.10.40 |
| Copers Cope Road | 12.9.40 night |
| Copers Cope Road | 25/26.9.40 |
| Copers Cope Road | 11/12.10.40 |
| Copers Cope Road Lloyds Bank Sports Ground | 20.1.43 |
| Copse Ave WW | 1/2.11.40 |
| Corkscrew Hill WW | 30.9.40 |

| Where | Date |
|---|---|
| Court Downs Rd jcn Wickham Rd | 16/17.4.41 |
| Courtenay Rd | 8.11.40 |
| Courtfield Rise WW | 7.10.40 night |
| Courtfield Rise WW | 1/2.11.40 |
| Crab Hill | 19/20.10.40 |
| Crease Park | 28.1.41 |
| Crescent Rd | 16/17.4.41 |
| Cromwell Road | 5.6.43 |
| Croydon Rd Recreation Ground Paddling Pool | 9.11.40 |
| Croydon Rd Recreation Ground | 16/17.4.41 |
| Croydon Rd Recreation Ground | 3.10.40 am |
| Croydon Road - Beckenham on German radio as target | 5.6.43 |
| Croydon Road | 8.11.40 |
| Croydon Road | 29.12.40 |
| Croydon Road WW | 28/29.10.40 |
| Croydon Road | 19.4.41 |
| Croydon Road no.27 WW | 8.9.40 |
| Crystal Palace Grounds | 28.11.40 |
| Crystal Palace Park Rd | 7/8.11.40 |
| Crystal Palace Park Rd | 16/17.4.41 |
| Crystal Palace Park Rd | 11.11.40 |
| Crystal Palace Park Rd | 18/19.10.40 |
| Crystal Palace Park Rd | 14.9.40 pm - 16.9.40 |
| Cyphers | 28/29.9.40 |
| Den Road | 19/20.10.40 |
| Den Road | 7.10.43 |
| Dulverton Rd | 16/17.4.41 |
| Dunbar Ave | 3.10.40 night |
| Durban Road | 12.9.40 |
| Durban Road | 5.6.43 |
| Durban Road | 29.11.40 |
| Durban Road | 22/23.9.40 |
| Durban Road (2) | 16/17.4.41 |
| Durham Ave | 20.3.41 |
| Durham Ave | 27.9.40 |
| Durham Ave | 16/17.4.41 |
| Durham Ave | 12.9.40 |
| Durham Rd | 11/12.10.40 |
| Durham Rd | 12.9.40 |
| Dykes Way | 11/12.10.40 |
| Dykes Way | 29.11.40 |
| Eden Park Avenue | 14.9.40 pm - 16.9.40 |
| Eden Park Avenue | 18/19.9.40 night |
| Eden Park Avenue | 7/8.11.40 |
| Eden Park Avenue | 1/2.11.40 |
| Eden Park Avenue | 1/2.11.40 |
| Eden Road | 7/8.11.40 |
| Eden Way | 12.9.40 night |
| Eden Way | 8.11.40 |
| Eden Way | 16/17.4.41 |
| Eden Way | 23/24.9.40 |
| Eden Way | 3.10.40 night |
| Elmers End Muirhead factory workers | 20.1.43 |
| Elmers End area | 19.1.41 |
| Elmers End cemetery | 10.5.41 |
| Elmers End Road | 8/9.10.40 |
| Elmers End Road | 14.9.40 pm - 16.9.40 |

| Where | Date |
|---|---|
| Elmers End Road | 7.9.40 night |
| Elwill Way | 13/14.10.40 |
| Elwill Way | 14.9.40 pm - 16.9.40 |
| Elwill Way | 7.10.43 |
| Faversham Rd | 12.1.41 |
| Faversham Rd | 12.1.41 |
| Felmingham Rd | 24/25.10.40 |
| Forest Ridge | 11.9.40 |
| Forest Ridge | 15.11.40 |
| Forster Road | 30.8.40 |
| Forster Road | 27.12.40 |
| Foxgrove Ave | 23/24.10.40 |
| Foxgrove Ave | 23/24.11.40 |
| Foxgrove Road | 15/16.10.40 |
| Foxgrove Road | 8.9.40 |
| Foxgrove Road | 7.10.40 night |
| Foxgrove Road | 29.12.40 |
| Foxgrove Road | 21.11.40 |
| Foxgrove Road (3) | 16/17.4.41 |
| Gates Green Rd WW | 16/17.4.41 |
| Glanfield Rd | 14.9.40 pm - 16.9.40 |
| Glebe Way WW | 18.10.43 |
| Goddard Rd | 7/8.11.40 |
| Goodhart Way | 6/7.9.40 |
| Goodhart Way | 16/17.4.41 |
| Greenways | 1/2.11.40 |
| Greenways | 3.10.40 am |
| Greenways | 15.11.40 |
| Greenways to Brackley Rd | 25.10.40 |
| Grosvenor Rd | 16/17.4.41 |
| Gwydor Rd | 14.9.40 pm - 16.9.40 |
| Hampden Avenue | 22/23.9.40 |
| Hampden Road | 30.8.40 |
| Hampden Road | 5.6.43 |
| Hardings Lane | 8.11.40 |
| Hartfield Crescent WW | 16/17.4.41 |
| Hartfield Crescent (The Dell) WW | 22.3.44 |
| Harvest Bank Rd WW | 16/17.4.41 |
| Hawes Down shelter | 13/14.10.40 |
| Hawes Lane WW | 1/2.11.40 |
| Hawes Lane WW | 15/16.10.40 |
| Hawes Lane WW | 21.11.40 |
| Hawkhurst Way WW | 1/2.11.40 |
| Hayes Chase WW | 1942 |
| Hayes Chase WW | 16/17.4.41 |
| Hayes Hill | 6/7.9.40 |
| Hayes Lane | 3.10.40 am |
| Hayes Lane | 14.9.40 pm - 16.9.40 |
| Hayes Mead WW | 1/2.11.40 |
| Hayes Way | 1/2.11.40 |
| Hayes Way | 3.10.40 am |
| Hayes Way | 6.11.40 |
| Hayes Way | 12.11.40 |
| Hayes Way | 7.10.43 |
| Hayne Road | 29.11.40 |
| Hayne Road | 12.9.40 night |
| Hayne Road | 3.10.40 am |
| Hayne Road | 9/10.10.40 |
| Heartsease Girl Guides Camp WW | 22/23.11.40 |

| Where | Date |
|---|---|
| High St., Beckenham | 12.9.40 |
| High St., Beckenham | 14.9.40 pm - 16.9.40 |
| High St., Beckenham | 25/26.9.40 |
| Hillside Rd | 11/12.10.40 |
| Holland Way WW | 20.3.41 |
| Kangley Bridge Rd Carbon Ribbon Factory | 26.8.40 |
| Kangley Bridge Road | 8.12.40 |
| Kangley Bridge Road | 7.9.40 night |
| Kelsey Park | 1/2.11.40 |
| Kelsey Park | 3.10.40 am |
| Kelsey Park Rd | 21/22.9.40 |
| Kelsey Park Rd Night Coventry attacked | 12.11.40 |
| Kelsey Park Rd | 14.9.40 pm - 16.9.40 |
| Kelsey Way | 11.9.40 |
| Kemerton Rd | 16/17.4.41 |
| Kendall Rd | 10.5.41 |
| Kent House area | 3.10.40 am |
| Kent House Lane | 12.9.40 night |
| Kent House Lane | 7.9.40 night |
| Kent House Road | 8.12.40 |
| Kent House Road | 12/13.10.40 |
| Kent House Road | 15/16.10.40 |
| Kent House Road | 29.11.40 |
| Kent House Road | 12.9.40 night |
| Kenwood Drive | 15.11.40 |
| Kenwood Drive | 17/18.9.40 night |
| Kenwood Drive | 6.11.40 |
| Kings Hall Rd | 20.3.41 |
| Kings Hall Road | 16/17.10.40 |
| Kingshall Road | 14.9.40 pm - 16.9.40 |
| Kingshall Road | 12.9.40 |
| Kingsway WW | 7.10.40 night |
| Kingsway | 20.1 43 |
| Kingswood Ave | 19.3.41 |
| Kingswood Rd | 20/21.9.40 night |
| Kingswood Rd | 10/11.10.40 |
| Knighton Park | 28.7.41 |
| Langley Ct WW | 23/24.10.40 |
| Langley Park Golf Course | 1/2.11.40 |
| Langley Rd | 7/8.11.40 |
| Langley Road | 10.3.41 |
| Langley Road | 3.10.40 am |
| Langley Way WW | 1/2.11.40 |
| Langley Way | 16/17.4.41 |
| Langley Way | 10.5.41 |
| Lawn Rd | 16/17.4.41 |
| Lawn Road - St Paul's Church | 18.11.40 |
| Lawrie Park Road | 14.9.40 pm - 16.9.40 |
| Lawrie Park Road | 20.1.1943 |
| Layhams Rd | 20.11.40 |
| Layhams Rd to Wickham Court Hotel | 26.10.40 |
| Lennard Road | 12.9.40 night |
| Lennard Road | 14.9.40 pm - 16.9.40 |
| Lennard Road (County School) | 23/24.9.40 |
| Lennard Road | 9/10.10.40 |
| Lennard Road | 8.11.40 |
| Lennard Road | 29.12.40 |
| Lennard Road | 26.8.40 |
| Lennard Road (2) | 28/29.9.40 |
| Lennard Road | 3.3.43 |
| Lime Tree Walk WW | 20.3.41 |
| Linden Grove | 7.9.40 night |
| Links Rd | 8.9.40 |
| Links Road WW | 7.10.40 night |
| Links Way | 16/17.4.41 |
| Lloyds Bank Sports Ground off Copers Cope Rd | 21.11.40 |
| Maberley Road | 19.1.41 |
| Mackenzie Rd | 14.9.40 pm - 16.9.40 |
| Mackenzie Rd | 8/9.10.40 |
| Madison Gns | 7.10.43 |
| Malmains Rd | 16/17.4.41 |
| Malmains Way | 19/20.10.40 |
| Manor Park Close WW | 16/17.4.41 |
| Manor Road | 21/22.9.40 |
| Manor Rd WW | 16/17.4.41 |
| Manor Road | 14.9.40 pm - 16.9.40 |
| Manor Way | 12/13.10.40 |
| Manor Way | 17/18.9.40 night |
| Manor Way | 13/14.10.40 |
| Manor Way | 3.10.40 am |
| Manor Way | 14.9.40 pm - 16.9.40 |
| Manor Way | 12.11.40 |
| Marian Vian Fields | 9/10.10.40 |
| Marian Vian School shelter | 11.1.41 |
| Marlow Road | 3.10.40 am |
| Marlow Road | 9/10.10.40 |
| Marlow Road | 14.9.40 pm - 16.9.40 |
| Mays Hill Road | 29.11.40 |
| Merlin Grove | 23/24.9.40 |
| Merlin Grove | 15.11.40 |
| Merlin Grove | 23/24.10.40 |
| Midland Bank Sports Ground (4) | 16/17.4.41 |
| Monks Orchard Rd (2) | 16/17.4.41 |
| Monks Orchard Rd (2) | 23.6.43 |
| Nash farm cottage WW | 22/23.11.40 |
| Newlands Park | 7.9.40 night |
| Newlands Park | 8.11.40 |
| Newlands Park, Wayne Tank Co | 9/10.9.40 |
| Oakland Ave | 4.10.40 night |
| Oaklands Ave WW | 22/23.11.40 |
| Oaklands Ave WW | 11.11.40 |
| Oakwood Ave | 12.9.40 night |
| Oakwood Avenue | 23/24.11.40 |
| Odeon Cinema | 7.10.40 night |
| Overbrae | 11/12.10.40 |
| Overbury Ave | 6.11.40 |
| Overbury Ave | 15.11.40 |
| Oyez Sports Ground | 1/2.11.40 |
| Parish Lane (2) | 14.9.40 pm - 16.9.40 |
| Parish Lane | 3.10.40 am |
| Park Hill Rd (4) | 16/17.4.41 |
| Park Langley Golf Course | 7.9.40 day |
| Park Langley Golf Course (3) | 16/17.4.41 |
| Park Road | 3.10.40 am |

| Where | Date |
|---|---|
| Park Road | 1/2.11.40 |
| Phoenix Rd | 14.9.40 pm - 16.9.40 |
| Pickhurst Lane WW | 6/7.9.40 |
| Pickhurst Lane WW | 7.10.40 night |
| Pickhurst Lane WW | 16/17.4.41 |
| Pickhurst Rise WW | 1/2.11.40 |
| Pickhurst Rise WW | 16/17.4.41 |
| Pickhurst Rise WW | 13/14.10.40 |
| Pickhurst Rise WW | 1/2.10.40 |
| Pickhurst Rise WW | 6/7.9.40 |
| Pickhurst Rise WW | 17/18.9.40 night |
| Pickhurst Rise WW | 10.5.41 |
| Piquet Rd | 14.9.40 pm - 16.9.40 |
| Pondfield Rd WW | 1/2.11.40 |
| Queen Anne Ave | 28/29.9.40 |
| Queen Anne Ave | 4.12.40 |
| Queens Road | 11.9.40 |
| Queensmead | 11/12.10.40 |
| Queensway WW | 16/17.4.41 |
| Queensway WW | 20.3.41 |
| Queensway WW | 11/12.10.40 |
| Queensway WW | 8.12.40 |
| Queensway WW | 7.10.40 night |
| Queensway WW | 25/26.9.40 |
| Ravensbourne Ave | 7.10.43 |
| Ravensbourne Ave | 19/20.10.40 |
| Ravensbourne Ave | 29.12.40 |
| Ravensbourne Ave | 7.10.40 night |
| Ravensbourne Ave (7) | 16/17.4.41 |
| Ravensbourne Road | 19.3.41 |
| Ravenscroft Rd | 12.9.40 night |
| Ravenscroft Rd | 26.10.40 |
| Ravensmead Road | 3.3.43 |
| Ravenswood Ave WW | 19.3.41 |
| Ravenswood Ave WW | 7.10.40 night |
| Ravenswood Ave WW | 10.3.41 |
| Ravenswood Crescent WW | 8.12.40 |
| Raymond Rd | 7/8.11.40 |
| Red Lodge Road WW | 1/2.11.40 |
| Reddons Road | 8.11.40 |
| Reddons Road | 12.9.40 night |
| Reddons Road | 7.9.40 night |
| Ridsdale Rd, Penge | 16/14.4.41 |
| Robbins Grove WW | 16/17.4.41 |
| Romanhurst Ave | 29.11.40 |
| Romanhurst Gardens | 14.9.40 pm - 16.9.40 |
| Romanhurst Gardens | 10/11.10.40 |
| Rouse farm WW | 28.11.40 |
| Rowden Rd | 14.9.40 pm - 16.9.40 |
| Royal Oak Laundry | 10.5.41 |
| Sandilands Crescent WW | 18.10.43 |
| Sandilands Crescent WW | 1942 |
| Sandilands Crescent and farm land WW | 29.10.40 |
| Scotts Lane | 7.10.40 day |
| Shaftesbury children's home WW | 7.9.40 day |
| Shaftesbury children's home WW | 28/29.10.40 |
| Shaftesbury Road | 11.9.40 |
| Sherwood Way WW | 1/2.11.40 |

| Where | Date |
|---|---|
| Sherwood Way WW | 8/9.10.40 |
| Shortlands Church St Mary's | 16/17.4.41 |
| Shortlands Grove | 8.9.40 |
| Shortlands Grove | 19/20.10.40 |
| Shortlands Station | 16/17.4.41 |
| Sidney Road | 10.5.41 |
| South Eden Park area | 6.1.41 |
| South Eden Park Rd | 1/2.11.40 |
| South Eden Park Rd | 12.9.40 |
| South Eden Park Rd | 5.1.41 |
| South Eden Road | 10.5.41 |
| South Hill Rd | 20.3.41 |
| South Walk WW | 18.10.43 |
| South Walk WW | 7.10.40 night |
| South Walk WW | 11/12.10.40 |
| Southend Rd | 3.10.40 am |
| Southend Rd | 12.9.40 night |
| Southend Rd | 16/17.4.41 |
| Southend Rd | 19/20.10.40 |
| Southend Rd no 6 demolished | 13.9.40 day |
| Southill Rd | 12.1.41 |
| Sparrows Den WW | 20.11.40 |
| Spring Park Woods WW | 10.3.41 |
| St James's Ave | 30.8.40 |
| St James's Ave | 25/26.9.40 |
| St James's Ave | 28/29.9.40 |
| St Margaret's Road | 10.5.41 |
| St Margaret's Road | 19.1.41 |
| St Margaret's Road | 7/8.11.40 |
| St Margaret's Road | 23/24.10.40 |
| St Margaret's Road (Villas) | 24/25.10.40 |
| St Margaret's Road (Villas) | 19.4.41 |
| Staffords garage WW | 16/17.4.41 |
| Stanhope Grove | 28.1.41 |
| Station Rd WW & around WW | 30.9.40 |
| Station Road W W | 14.9.40 pm - 16.9.40 |
| Station Road, Penge | 11.1.41 |
| Station Road, Penge | 12.9.40 |
| Stone Park Ave | 14.9.40pm - 16.9.40 |
| Stone Park Ave | 28.1.41 |
| Surrey Road WW | 20.1.43 |
| Sydenham Road | 3.3.43 |
| Sylvan Way WW | 31.1.41 |
| Tennyson Rd | 19/20.9.40 night |
| Thayers Farm Rd | 14.9.40 pm - 16.9.40 |
| Thayers Farm Rd | 11.9.40 |
| The Avenue | 21.11.40 |
| The Avenue | 19/20.10.40 |
| The Avenue | 15/16.10.40 |
| The Avenue | 7.10.40 night |
| The Avenue | 28/29.9.40 |
| The Avenue (4) | 16/17.4.41 |
| The Crescent WW | 28/29.10.40 |
| The Knoll | 21/22.9.40 |
| The Knoll | 8.9.40 |
| The Mead WW | 1/2.11.40 |
| The Mead (2) WW | 16/17.4.41 |
| The Warren WW | 18.10.43 |
| Thesiger Rd | 28.7.41 |

| Where | Date |
|---|---|
| Thesiger Rd | 8.11.40 |
| Thicket Rd no. 10a | 23.2.44 |
| Tiepigs Lane WW | 6/7.9.40 |
| Tiepigs Lane (Clenstone) WW | 3.1.44 |
| Tudor Road | 26.9.40 am |
| Uplands | 11.9.40 |
| Upper Elmers Rd | 8.11.40 |
| Venner Road | 27.12.40 |
| Venner Road | 11.1.41 |
| Venner Road | 14.9.40 pm - 16.9.40 |
| Venner Road | 14.9.40 pm - 16.9.40 |
| Venner Road | 8.11.40 |
| Victor Rd | 19/20.9.40 night |
| Village Way | 20/21.10.40 |
| Village Way | 14.9.40 pm - 16.9.40 |
| Village Way | 1/2.11.40 |
| Village Way | 11.9.40 |
| Village Way | 1/2.11.40 |
| Warwick Rd | 8.11.40 |
| Well Wood WW | 9.3.41 |
| Wellcome's Fields | 17.10.40 |
| Wellcome Labs | 16/17.10.40 |
| West Wickham High St WW | 7.10.40 night |
| Westgate Rd | 23/24.11.40 |
| Westgate Rd | 16/17.4.41 |
| Westland Drive WW | 1/2.11.40 |
| Westmoreland Drive WW | 18.10.43 |
| Westmoreland Road | 20.3.41 |
| Westmoreland Road | 16/17.4.41 |
| Westmoreland Road | 12.9.40 |
| Westmoreland Road | 14.9.40 pm - 16.9.40 |
| Westmoreland Road | 8.12.40 |
| Whateley Rd | 8.11.40 |
| Whitecroft Way | 3.10.40 am |
| Whitecroft Way | 12.11.40 |
| Whitecross Way | 6.11.40 |
| Wickham Chase WW | 13/14.10.40 |
| Wickham Chase WW | 19.4.41 |

| Where | Date |
|---|---|
| Wickham Chase WW | 6.11.40 |
| Wickham Chase WW | 1/2.11.40 |
| Wickham Chase WW | 1/2.11.40 |
| Wickham Chase (2) WW | 16/17.4.41 |
| Wickham Court Fields WW | 16/17.10.40 |
| Wickham Court Fields WW | 17.10.40 |
| Wickham Rd | 19/20.10.40 |
| Wickham Rd | 26.9.40 am |
| Wickham Rd (3) | 16/17.4.41 |
| Wickham Way | 7.10.43 |
| Wickham Way | 1/2.11.40 |
| Wickham Way | 21/22.10.40 |
| Wickham Way | 10.11.40 |
| Wickham Way | 15.3.41 |
| Winchester Park | 7.10.43 |
| Winchester Rd | 11/12.10.40 |
| Windermere Rd WW | 15/16.10.40 |
| Witham Rd | 14.9.40 pm - 16.9.40 |
| Witham Rd | 10.5.41 |
| Wood Lodge Lane WW | 20.11.40 |
| Woodbastwick Rd | 8.12.40 |
| Woodbastwick Rd | 9.3.41 |
| Woodland Way WW | 17/18.9.40 night |
| Woodland Way WW | 22/23.11.40 |
| Woodmere Way | 21/22.10.40 |
| Worsley Bridge Road | 17.10.40 |
| Worsley Bridge Road | 20/21.9.40 night |
| Worsley Bridge Road | 16/17.10.40 |
| Worsley Bridge Road | 20.1.1943 |
| WW High St WW | 8/9.10.40 |
| WW High St WW | 1/2.11.40 |
| WW Station WW | 1/2.11.40 |
| Yoko Field & Ry Line | 26.8.40 |
| Z Miscellaneous 1 | 16/17.9.40 night |
| Z West Wickham area | 5.2.41 |
| Z West Wickham generally | 11.1.41 |

## A-Z list of roads bombed in Penge in the blitz

| Address | Date | Fatalities |
|---|---|---|
| Anerley Park 10 | 12.10.40 | Sophia Augusta Smith (93) |
| Anerley Park 10 | 12.10.40 | James Crabb (50) |
| Anerley Park 10 | 12.10.40 | Margaret Helen (10) |
| Anerley Park 10 | 12.10.40 | Louisa Dance (8) |
| Anerley Rd 150 | 3.11.40 | Evelyn Muirhead (64) |
| Anerley Rd 226 | 25.3.44 | Mary Wyatt (96) d Farnboro hosp |
| Anerley Rd 228 | 25.3.44 | John Cassidy (40) |
| Anerley Rd shelter | 9.10.40 | Kate Whyman (56) |
| Anerley Rd Shelter | 9.10.40 | George Victor Ebberson (32) |
| Anerley Rd Shelter | 9.10.40 | Mabel Teresa Gold (58) |
| Anerley Rd Shelter | 9.10.40 | Richard Arthur Gold (58) |
| Anerley Rd Shelter | 9.10.40 | Agnes Hamerston (67) |
| Anerley Rd Shelter | 9.10.40 | Charles Henry Hone (58) |
| Anerley Rd Shelter | 9.10.40 | Charles Howell (64) |
| Anerley Rd Shelter | 9.10.40 | Catherine Mahoney (29) |
| Anerley Rd Shelter | 9.10.40 | Alfred Preston (55) |
| Bourdon Rd 23 | 8.10.40 | Charles Sydney Thomas Frankling (40) |
| Cambridge Grove | 29.12.40 | Minnie Hunt (53) |
| Cambridge Grove | 29.12.40 | Dorothy May Vockins (19) |
| Croydon Rd 109 | 8.10.40 | Frederick Harold Gater (19) |
| High St | 6.11.40 | Edward Alfred Baines (19) |
| High St | 6.11.40 | William John Bowyer (29) |
| Howard Rd 4 | 17.10.40 | Constance Allen (71) |
| Kingsdale Rd 31 | 7.11.40 | Harold Leo Pearman |
| Maberley Crescent 2 | 24.10.40 | William Henry Allsop (61) |
| Madeline Rd 1 | 3.11.40 | Hannah Bunn (80) |
| Oakfield Rd 102 | 12.9.40 | Florence Martha Skellorn (62) |
| Oakfield Rd 102 | 12.9.40 | Thomas Hugh Skellorn (65) |
| Oakfield Rd 102 | 12.8.40 | Alfred James Elkins (42) |
| Oakfield Rd 102 | 12.9.40 | Elizabeth Ann Elkins (5) |
| Oakfield Rd 102 | 12.9.40 | Gladys Florence Elkins (40) |
| Queen Adelaide Rd 16 | 15.9.40 | Ernest Charles Riches (65) |
| Ridsdale Rd 48 | 16.4.41 | Charlotte Llewellyn (57) |
| Ridsdale Rd 48 | 16.4.41 | Arthur Ben Churchman (68) |
| Ridsdale Rd 50 | 16.4.41 | John Johnstone Holliday (66) |
| Ridsdale Rd 50 | 16.4.41 | Nellie Cooper (57) |
| St John's Rd 8 | 15.9.40 | Ida Elsie Carder (51) |
| St John's Rd 8 | 15.9.40 | Maggie Evelyn Carpenter (4) |
| St John's Rd 8 | 15.9.40 | Emma Pengelly |
| Wiverton Rd 55 | 6.11.40 | Edward Henry Watson (33) |
| Worbeck Rd 7 | 8.10.40 | John Henry Michael Porter (22m) |

The Anerley Road Shelter was opposite Maple Road.

# Flying bomb and rocket fatalities in and attacks on Beckenham

132 killed, 1085 injured, 1013 houses destroyed, 1600 damaged
73 Doodlebugs on Beckenham borough (includes WW but not Penge)

| | | |
|---|---|---|
| Abbots Way | | 3.8.44 |
| Addington Rd | Rose Anna Rebecca Earl (68) at public shelter | 21.6.44 |
| Albemarle Rd | Gladys Pretoria Mooney (44), Harry Mooney (45), Patrick John Mooney (15), at 7 | 2.7.44 |
| Albemarle/Westgate Rd | | 10.8.44 |
| Altyre Way | | 30.6.44 |
| Barnfield Wood Rd | Edgar Clarence Law (69), Maggie Law (66), of 63 | 22.7.44 |
| 199 Beckenham Rd at Mrs Richards' restaurant | Alfred Albert Awcock (40), David Adam Bidmead (46), Edward George Brooks (50), Margaret Chegwidden (30), Valerie Ann Chegwidden (5), Stanley Herbert Childs (32), Francis Edward Clark (40), Margaret Hilda Crozier (30), Alfred Edward Girdler (40), Sidney Ephraim Hancock (50), Frederick Ingles (68), Alfred George King (38), Henry Liddle Lamb (39), Arthur Maskell (51), Home Guard Maurice Charles Mitchell (19), Reginald Quittenton (42), Bert Raper (18), Walter Thomas Reynolds (30), Albert Thomas Richards (58), Arthur Henry Smith (62), Marion Solans (36), Herbert Steer (56), Florence Trindall (38), Pamela Trindall (13), Arthur Stanley Warburton (27), Ellen Florence Webb (71), Frederick William Whitmey (41), Warden Frank Woolward (21). | 2.8.44 |
| Beckenham Rd | Ernest George Burgon (49), John William Darkin (59), Albert Henry Elliott (37), Frank William Eldridge (36), Walter Gorham (25), Warden Titus Hadlington (44) George Richard Harwood (39), Samson Sade (61). | 2.8.44 |
| 203 Beckenham Rd | Minnie Rust (73), Minnie Rust (51), tailors | 2.8.44 |
| 197 Beckenham Rd | Edwin Fitch (73), grocer | 2.8.44 |
| 195 Beckenham Rd | Sidney Ephraim Hancock (50) and Richard Carpenter (62) fishmongers | 2.8.44 |
| 117, Beckenham Rd | Adelaide Alice Killick (57), | 2.8.44 |
| Bethlem Grounds | Luke Morgan (72), at Evening Standard Sports ground - Eden Way | 16.6.44 |
| Bethlem Grounds | One of several - also recorded as Croydon | 27.6.44 |
| Blakes Rec | | 3.8.44 |
| Blandford Rd | Ann Mary Edlin, (9m), of 16 | 1.7.44 |
| Bramerton Rd | Albert Victor Collens (61), Lilian Mary Collens (61), Joan Sylvia Collens (20), at 36, Charles Ellman Smith (66), Maud Ellen Smith (65) of 34 | 27.7.44 |
| Bramerton Rd | | 2.8.44 |
| Cator Park | | 5.7.44 |
| Cator Park | | 22.7.44 |
| Cherry Tree Walk | George Frederick Handel (45) of 14 | 4.8.44 |
| Church Rd | Ernest Day (66) of 8, Eveline (75) and Thomas Gasson (73) of 7, | 28.7.44 |
| Copers Cope Rd | Evelyn Kennaway (71), of 31 | 1.7.44 |
| Crampton Rd | Graham Henry Baker (18), at 90, Emily Ellen Clare (64), at 119, Alfred John Strudwick (62), at 86 | 22.6.44 |
| Crystal Palace Park Rd (Border Rd) | | 3.8.44 |
| Downs Hill Rd | | 20.8.44 |
| Croydon Rd, Elmers End industrial estate | John Barry Bentley (25). (seen by Tony Johns, J B Bentley jumped off his bike into landing flybomb). Joan Ottoway (24), Amelia Mary Spindler (55), at Elmers End Rd shelter? | 18.7.44 |

| Location | Details | Date |
|---|---|---|
| 36 Elmers End Road | Arthur Spence (83) of 103 | 12.7.44 |
| Elmers End Road Bus Garage | Ellen Burton, John Edward Cunningham (54), Florence Elliott (60), Heavy Rescue Leonard George (42), Florence Eugenie Grey (47), Kenneth Alfred Percy Homden (20), (injured died next day), Herbert James Hutchins (51), Herbert William Leach, (50), Florence Rarp (32), Thomas William Sharpe (44), Walter James Singlehurst (62), Michael Eugene Smyth (28), Charles Stares (52), Sydney Arthur Steer (17), Frank William Stevens (32), Alfred John Wilbourn (50). | 18.7.44 |
| Elwill Way | | 22.7.44 |
| Goddard Rd | | 22.7.44 |
| High St WW | Eileen Florence Jeffery, (24), | 11.7.44 |
| Hong Kong Bank Ground | | 22.7.44 |
| Kelsey Park | | 2.8.44 |
| Kemerton Rd | | 3.8.44 |
| Kent House Lane | | 21.7.44 |
| Kent House Rd | Maude Adams (72), of 226 | 14.7.44 |
| Kingshall/Aldersmead Rd | William Edward Hazelgrove (68), of 58, Kate Smith (7), of 56, Carl Henry Young (47), at 54. | 2.7.44 |
| Kingswood Ave | Oliver Frederick Stanley, (58), at 79, died 13.8. fell Druids Way | 3.8.44 |
| Lawrie Park Rd | Mary Ethelreda Dujardyn, (48), Raymond Theodore Dujardyn, (47), of 54 Park Court, Jessie Constance Tate, 60 at 50 Park Court. | 1.8.44 |
| Layhams Rd, May Farm | | 2.8.44 |
| Lennard Rd | | 30.6.44 |
| Links Rd, all Heavy Rescue | Ernest Stanley Agate (24), Henry John Bailey (50), Harold Albert Browne (33), Frank William Burton (40), Lawrence Walter Lathwood (54), George Victor Wingham (58), At 10 Links Rd, Fred Goodchild (70) was injured and died 27.6. at Beckenham hospital. | 16.6.44 |
| Maberley Rd | | 3.7.44 |
| Mackenzie Rd | | 30.6.44 |
| Meadway | | 23.6.44 |
| Merlin Grove | On empty POW camp | 16.6.44 |
| Nash Lane | | 27.6.44 |
| Nat Prov Ground | | 7/8.44 |
| Nat Prov Ground | Witness by PM | 5.1.45 |
| Oakwood Ave | Ada Elizabeth Edwards (70), of 14 | 30.7.44 |
| Park Langley golf course | | 10.7.44 |
| Queens Rd (2) | Emily Agnes Johnson (58), at 71, Ellen Naomi Whitehead (35), Sylvia Pamela Whitehead (18m), at 73 | 21.6.44 |
| Queens Rd | | 26.8.44 |
| Queens Rd | | 5.7.44 |
| Queens Rd | | 26.8.44 |
| Rectory Rd | Albert Edward Codling (45), | 28.6.44 |
| St James's Ave | 17-24 | 26.7.44 |
| St Mary's Church | Kingswood Rd / Church Rd | 22.7.44 |
| St Mary's Church & Vicarage | St. Mary's Ave / Church Rd | 27.7.44 |
| Shortlands Rd | Ellen Catherine Child (48), at 75, Sarah Constance Reichwald, (73), at 42, died 6.7. | 28.6.44 |
| Shortlands Rd | | 29.6.44 |
| South Eden Park Road | | 20.7.44 |
| South Eden Park Road | (BPGS) Boys School playing fields | 31.8.44 |
| Sparrows Den | | 27.7.44 |
| The Avenue, Beckenham | Mabel Alexandra Merrick (38), at 64 | 17.6.44 |
| The Alders | | 28.6.44 |

| | | |
|---|---|---|
| The Drive | John Bowles Adams (70), of 72A, (died on 26.6)<br>Annie Florence Dallaway (43), of 77 (died on 25.6),<br>Dorothy Jennie Knight (50), of 82 (died on 26.6) | 25.6.44 |
| The Grove | Tyler Norman (72), at 21 | 12.7.44 |
| Thesiger Rd | | |
| Tootswood Rd | George Ripley (46), Florence Seath (38),<br>Reginald Allen Seath (37) | 16.6.44 |
| Westfield Rd | Susan Bloice (63), of 22, Annie Elizabeth Constable (66), at 13,<br>William Ginn (78), Norman George Robert Partridge (44), at 17 | 23.6.44 |
| Wickham Chase | | 17.6.44 |
| Wickham Ct Farm | | 28.6.44 |
| Wickham Ct Farm | | 1.7.44 |
| Wickham Ct Farm | | 29.7.44 |
| Wickham Rd | | |
| Christchurch area | Frederick John Bunting (53), Burnhill Rd<br>Charles Edward Castle (48), Fairfield Rd<br>Gladys Belle Cotton (52), Burnhill Rd<br>Ada Crossthwaite (75), Burnhill Rd<br>Alice Mary Ann Fane (58), Lea Rd<br>Richard Green (83), Burnhill Rd<br>Beatrice Jane Lane (5), at 1 Lea Rd<br>Frank Norman (80), Lea Rd<br>Louisa Norman (84), Lea Rd<br>John Frederick Radford (49), Kelsey Park Rd<br>Arthur William Smith (55), Fairfield Rd<br>Cecil Wingrove (51) Fairfield Rd | 5.1.45 |

## V2 Rockets. Five fell on Beckenham (see p50)
### Fatalities occured only from that which fell in Crystal Palace Park Rd

| | | |
|---|---|---|
| 75 Crystal Palace Park Rd | Anne Georgina Elisa Jones (64),<br>Edward Michael Jones (65), | 15.3.45 |
| 73 Crystal Palace Park Rd | Elizabeth Kimpton (69),<br>Gertrude Marguarete Phillips (23),<br>Richard Walter Phillips (22),<br>Dorothy Grace Philp (47),<br>Edwin Cedric Stewart Pillow (16),<br>Marguerita Frances Pillow (46),<br>Ada Woods (61). | |

NB. The V1 incidents appear to total more than 73, because several which fell in fields were not recorded.

## Flying bomb fatalities in Penge

| | | |
|---|---|---|
| Anerley Park 5 | 18.6.44 | Ada Emma Eldridge (76) |
| Anerley Park 5 | 18.6.44 | Florence Mary Newton (55) |
| Anerley Rd | 11.7.44 | Frances Ivy Jean Bradley (24) |
| Anerley Rd | 11.7.44 | George Robertson Carns (69) |
| Anerley Rd | 11.7.44 | Elsie Maud Davies (44) |
| Anerley Rd | 11.7.44 | George Steven Smith (14) |
| Anerley Rd | 11.7.44 | Lily Elsie Smith (32) |
| Anerley Rd | 11.7.44 | Maurice John Stedman (13) |
| Anerley Rd | 11.7.44 | William Henry King (57) |
| Anerley Rd 15 | 11.7.44 | Kathleen Fanny Elizabeth Coppin (40) |
| Anerley Rd 66 | 11.7.44 | Eric John Dove (11) |
| Belvedere Rd 57 | 10.7.44 | Annie Marshment (63) |
| Belvedere Rd 53 | 10.7.44 | Edith Lavinia Aldred (60) |
| Belvedere Rd 53 | 10.7.44 | Kate Sims (75) |
| Belvedere Rd 57 | 10.7.44 | Valerie Roythorne (9) |
| Blenheim Rd 3 | 21.7.44 | Winifred Amy Bryant (18) |
| Blenheim Rd 7 | 21.7.44 | Arthur Carter (79) |
| Blenheim Rd 7 | 21.7.44 | Elizabeth Carter (76) |
| Blenheim Rd 7 | 21.7.44 | Elizabeth Carter (36) |
| Blenheim Rd 7 | 21.7.44 | William Carter (40) |
| Cottingham Rd 7 | 29.6.44 | Edith Watts (49) Air raid warden |
| Cottingham Rd 7 | 29.6.44 | John Alan Watts (17) |
| Crystal Palace Station Rd | 11.7.44 | Charles Norton Dale (60) |
| High St 110 | 21.7.44 | Frank Thorpe (51) |
| High St 26 | 18.6.44 | Harry Charles Scholfield (57) |
| High St 28 | 18.6.44 | Sidney P Gee |
| High St 30 | 18.6.44 | Nellie Cooper (68) |
| High St 30 | 18.6.44 | Shem Cooper (70) |
| High St 32 | 18.6.44 | Arthur Ransome Ball (39) |
| High St 32 | 18.6.44 | Emily Ball (30) |
| High St 32 | 18.6.44 | Janet Maureen Ball (3m) |
| High St 32 | 18.6.44 | Florence Mabel Bengerfield (62) |
| High St 32 | 18.6.44 | Rachel Burrows (64) |
| High St 32 | 18.6.44 | Edward Henry Long (48) |
| High St 32 | 18.6.44 | Elizabeth Minnie Patman (67) |
| Laurel Grove 80 | 29.6.44 | Alan Coventry Barber (16) |
| Laurel Grove 80 | 29.6.44 | Reginald Leslie Barber (15) |
| Laurel Grove 80 | 29.6.44 | George Hamilton Barber |
| Oak Grove Rd 40 | 30.6.44 | Rose Wells (57) |
| Oak Grove Rd 42 | 30.6.44 | Ellen Susan Jarvis (51) |
| Oak Grove Rd 48 | 30.6.44 | Lillian Kathleen Skegg (36) |
| Palace Square 13 | 10.7.44 | Frances Wixey (35) |
| Palace Square 13 | 10.7.44 | Kate Julia Wixey (67) |
| Palace Square 19 | 10.7.44 | George Stenhouse (42) |
| Palace Square 19 | 10.7.44 | Patricia Diana Stenhouse (9) |
| Ridgemount Close 2 | 13.7.44 | William Butler (64) |
| Ridgemount Close 4 | 13.7.44 | Dennis Field (12) |
| Thicket Grove 8 | 26.7.44 | James Foster (64) |
| Trenholme Rd 17 | 2.7.44 | Patricia Mary Phillips (16) |
| Trenholme Rd 17 | 2.7.44 | Winifred Mary Teresa Phillips (52) |
| Trenholme Rd 18 | 2.7.44 | Emily Foster (70) |
| Trenholme Rd 18 | 2.7.44 | Joseph Stanley Vickers 33 fireman |
| Trenholme Rd 18 | 2.7.44 | Michael David Vickers (7) |
| Trenholme Rd 18 | 2.7.44 | Patrick Anthony Vickers (8) |
| Trenholme Rd 18 | 2.7.44 | Vera Christina Vickers (31) |
| Trenholme Rd 19 | 2.7.44 | Lucy Savidge (55) |
| Trenholme Rd 19 | 2.7.44 | Nathan Savidge (70) |
| Trenholme Rd 21 | 2.7.44 | Joan Iris Field (16) |
| Trenholme Rd 37 | 2.7.44 | Lily Florence Ray (40) |
| Trenholme Rd 38 | 2.7.44 | Margaret Philemon Bezer (33) |
| Wordsworth Rd 38 | 3.8.44 | Alice May Webb (50) |
| Wordsworth Rd 42 | 3.8.44 | William John Terry (71) |

Note: No V2 rockets fell on Penge

# Beckenham blitz incidents and numbers of casualties

| Day | Date | | Where | What | Casualties |
|-----|------|---|-------|------|------------|
| Mon | 26.8.40 | | Yoko Field & Ry Line, Lennard Rd | Bombs | None |
| Mon | 26.8.40 | | Kangley Bridge Rd Carbon ribbon factory | | |
| Fri | 30.8.40 | | Corner Clockhouse Rd & Hampden Rd, Hampden Rd, St James's Ave, Forster Rd | Bombs | 3 killed, Michael Glenny (9), trapped 1.5 hrs |
| Fri/Sat | 6/7.9.40 | | Tiepigs Lane, Coney Hall Rec, Hayes Hill, Broadoaks way, Pickhurst Lane, Goodhart Way, Abbots Way, Pickhurst Rise, Bourne Way | HE & incendiaries | None |
| Sat | 7.9.40 | | Shaftesbury children's home, WW | Unexploded bomb | None |
| | 7.9.40 | day | Park Langley Golf course | Hurricane crashed on fire | pilot escaped |
| | 7.9.40 | night | Newlands Park | | 4 killed 12 injured |
| | 7.9.40 night | | Linden Grove | | 3 injured |
| | 7.9.40 night | | Reddons Rd, Kangley Bridge Rd, Elmers End Rd, Kent House Lane | | None |
| Sun | 8.9.40 | | Wardens post 57 at 27 Croydon Rd WW demolished | oil bomb & HE | 7 wardens escaped unhurt |
| | 8.9.40 | | The Knoll, Shortlands Grove, Foxgrove Rd, Links Rd | Bombs | None |
| Mon/Tues | 9/10.9.40 | | Newlands Park, Wayne Tank Co | Incendiaries | None |
| Wed | 11.9.40 | | Kelsey Way, Uplands, Forest Ridge, Village Way, Shaftesbury Rd, Queens Rd, Clockhouse Rd, Thayers Farm Rd | Sticks of bombs | 1 killed, 5 injured overall on 11th |
| Wed | 11.9.40 | | Durban Rd, Westmoreland Rd, Station Rd Penge, Kingshall Rd, High St, South Eden Park Rd. | Bombs | None |
| Wed | 11.9.40 | | Durham Rd, Durham Ave | Oil bomb | None |
| Thurs | 12.9.40 | night | Kent House Lane, Reddons Rd, Copers Cope Rd, Barnfield Wood Rd, Brackley Rd, Eden Way, Hayne Rd, Lennard Rd, Kent House Rd, Coney Hall Rec, Oakwood Ave, Southend Rd, St Paul's Church, Ravenscroft Rd | | None |
| Fri | 13.9.40 | day | 6 Southend Rd demolished, damage over wide area of Beckenham and West Wickham | HE & incendiaries | 8 killed, 5 injured |
| Sat, until Monday 16.9.40 longest raid | 14.9.40 | pm | Nursing home at 19 Crystal Palace, Romanhurst Gns, Station Rd WW, Braemar Gns, Ravenswood Ave, West Wickham High St, Beckenham Rd, Kingshall Rd, Westmoreland Rd, Venner Rd, Marlow Rd, Clockhouse Rd, Stone Park Ave, Hayes Lane, Piquet Rd, Witham Rd, Glanfield Rd, Mackenzie Rd, Ancaster Rd, Gwydor Rd, Arrol Rd, Cherry Tree Walk, Elwill Way, Barnfield Wood Rd, Eden Park Ave, Cedars Rd, Lawrie Park Rd, High St, Phoenix Rd, Kelsey Park Rd, Thayers Farm Rd, Parish Lane, Brackley Rd, Venner Rd, Elmers End Rd, Lennard Rd, Parish Lane, Manor Rd, Rowden Rd, Village Way, Manor Way | | 23 killed 37 injured |

| Day | Date | | Where | What | Casualties |
|---|---|---|---|---|---|
| Wed | 18/19.9.40 | night | Bramerton Rd, Eden Park Ave | | |
| Thurs | 19/20.9.40 | night | Victor Rd, Tennyson Rd | | 7 killed, 25 injured |
| Fri | 20/21.9.40 | night | Kingswood Rd | Parachute mine | |
| Fri | 20/21.9.40 | | Worsley Bridge Rd | HE | |
| Sat | 21/22.9.40 | | Manor Rd, Kelsey Park, The Knoll" | Bombs | |
| Sun | 22/23.9.40 | | Hampden Ave, Durban Rd, Belmont Rd, Cedars Rd | | 5 killed, 15 injured |
| Mon | 23/24.9.40 | | Eden Way, Merlin Grove | Incendiaries | |
| Mon | 23/24.9.40 | | Unexploded time bombs damaged trenches (shelters) of Girls Grammar School in Lenard Road | | |
| Tues | 25/26.9.40 | | St James's Ave, High St, Copers Cope Rd | Ack-ack shells | |
| Wed | 25/26.9.40 | | Queensway, WW | plane crashed | |
| Thurs | 26.9.40 | am | Tudor Rd, Wickham Rd | | 1 Killed, 2 injured |
| Fri | 27.9.40 | | Durham Ave | | 2 killed |
| Sat | 28/29.9.40 | | Queen Anne Ave, Lennard Rd, Cyphers, St James's Ave, The Avenue, Lennard Rd, Copers Cope Rd" | HE and AA shells | 4 killed |
| Mon | 30.9.40 | | Round W W station, Corkscrew Hill | Bombs | 3 killed |
| Tues | 1/2.10.40 | | Ashleigh Rd | Unexploded bomb | |
| Tues | 1/2.10.40 | | Pickhurst Rise | Bombs | 3 injured |
| Thurs | 3.10.40 | am | Croydon Rd Recreation ground | Incendiaries | |
| Thurs | 3.10.40 | | Kent House area | Incendiaries | |
| Thurs | 3.10.40 | | Brackley Rd | 3 oil bombs | |
| Thurs | 3.10.40 | | Marlow Rd, Langley Rd, Blakeney Rd, Southend Rd, Hayes Way, Manor Way, Greenways, Whitecroft Way, Kelsey Park, Brabourne Rise, Park Rd, Hayes Lane, Hayne Rd, Parish Lane | HEs | |
| Thurs | 3.10.40 | night | Dunbar Ave, Eden Way | | |
| Fri | 4.10.40 | night | Oakland Ave | Cannon shell | |
| Mon | 7.10.40 | day | Scotts Lane | Oil bomb | |
| Mon | 7.10.40 | night | West Wickham High St, Odeon cinema, Links Rd, Ravenswood Ave, South Walk, Queensway, Kingsway, Courtfield Rise, Addington Rd, Pickhurst Lane. | | |
| Mon | | | Bromley Rd, Foxgrove Rd, The Avenue, Ravensbourne Ave, Albemarle Rd (2) | | |
| Tues | 8/9.10.40 | night | Elmers End Rd, Mackenzie Rd Sherwood Way, WW High St | | 1 killed, 30 injured |
| Wed | 9/10.10.40 | night | Marlow Rd, Lennard Rd, Clockhouse Rd | | 3 killed |
| Wed | 9/10.10.40 | night | Hayne Rd, Copers Cope Rd, Marian Vian Fields | Incendiaries | |
| Thurs | 10/11.10.40 | night | Kingswood Rd, Romanhurst Gns | | |
| Fri | 11/12.10.40 | | Queensmead, Dykes Way, Hillside Rd, Overbrae, Winchester Rd, Durham Rd, Braeside, Copers Cope Rd, South Walk, Addington Rd, Queensway | | |
| Sat | 12/13.10.40 | | Manor Way, Kent House Rd" | Unexploded bomb | |
| Sun | 13/14.10.40 | | Pickhurst Rise, Barnfield Wood Rd, Elwill Way, Bushey Way, Wickham Chase | | |
| Sun | 13/14.10.40 | | Hawes Down shelter | 1 injured | |
| Tues | 15/16.10.40 | | Foxgrove Rd, The Avenue, Hawes Lane | Oil bombs | |
| Tues | 15/16.10.40 | | Kent House Rd, Windemere Rd | HEs | 3 killed |

| Day | Date | | Where | What | Casualties |
|-----|------|---|-------|------|------------|
| Wed | 16/17.10.40 | | Cator Park, Kingshall Rd, Worsley Bridge Rd, Wellcome labs, Wickham Court fields | | |
| Thurs | 17.10.40 | | Wickham Court fields | 10 to 12 bombs | |
| Thurs | 17.10.40 | | Cator Rd | Parachute mine | |
| Thurs | 17.10.40 | | Worsley Bridge Rd, Cator Park, Wellcome's fields | Bombs | |
| Fri | 18/19.10.40 | | Crystal Palace Park Rd by Thicket Rd | | Percy Crease inj |
| Sat | 19/20.10.40 | | Wickham Rd, Southend Rd, Barnfield Wood Rd, Den Rd, Shortlands Grove, Malmains Way, Broomfield Rd, Ravensbourne Ave | HEs | 4 killed, 8 injured |
| Sat | 19/20.10.40 | | The Avenue, Crab Hill | Oil bombs | |
| Sun | 20/21.10.40 | | Birkbeck Rd, Beckenham Rd, Village Way | | 3 killed, 17 injured |
| Mon | 21/22.10.40 | | Bolderwood Way, Wickham Way, Brabourne Rise, Woodmere Way | | |
| Wed | 23/24.10.40 | | Foxgrove Ave | | Gammons killed |
| Wed | 23/24.10.40 | | St Margaret's Rd, Merlin Grove, Langley Ct, Coney Hall | | |
| Fri | 24/25.10.40 | | Felmingham Rd, St Margaret's Villas | | 1 killed |
| Sat | 25.10.40 | night | Greenways to Brackley Rd | String bombs | |
| Sun | 26.10.40 | | Layhams Rd to Wickham Court Hotel | Messerschmidt Pilot baled out | |
| Sun | 26.10.40 | | Ravenscroft Rd | Unexploded bomb | |
| Tues | 28/29.10.40 | | Shaftesbury Homes | | 2 staff killed, the cook and a maid |
| Tues | 28/29.10.40 | | The Crescent, Croydon Rd, Abbotsbury Rd | | |
| Wed | 29.10.40 | | Sandilands Crescent and farm land | Oil bomb, HEs | |
| Fri | 1/2.11.40 | | WW High St, Bolderwood Way, Hawkhurst Way, Copse Ave, Sherwood Way, Wickham Chase, Langley Way, Pickhurst Rise, Hayes Mead, Pondfield Rd | Incendiaries | |
| Fri | 1/2.11.40 | | WW station, Red Lodge Rd, Eden Park Ave, Cator Rd, Wickham Way, Hayes Way, South Eden Park Rd, Bourne Way, Addington Rd, Courtfield Rise, Hawes Lane, Coney Hall Rec, Westland Drive, Wickham Chase, The Mead, Langley Park Golf Course, Kelsey Park, Village Way | HEs | |
| Fri | 1/2.11.40 | | Village Way, Greenways, Eden Park Ave, Oyez sports ground, Park Rd | Oil bombs | |
| Sat | 11/02/1940 | am | Brackley Rd at Southend Rd | One large bomb demolished house | |
| | 11/06/1940 | | Hayes Way, Bushey Way, Overbury Ave, Kenwood Drive, Whitecroft, Brabourne Rise | | |
| | 11/06/1940 | night | Bushey Way, Wickham Chase | | 1 killed |
| Fri | 7/8.11.40 | | Eden Rd, Eden Park Ave, Balmoral Ave, Raymond Rd, Crystal Palace Park Rd, Goddard Rd, Langley Rd, Blandford Rd, Beckenham Rd, Clockhouse Rd, Elmers End, St Margaret's Rd, Beckenham Rugby Football Club | | |

| Day | Date | Where | What | Casualties |
|---|---|---|---|---|
| Evening | 8.11.40 | Beckenham PO, Warwick Rd, Thesiger Rd, Venner Rd, Upper Elmers End Rd, Hardings Lane, Eden Way, Reddons Rd, Courtenay Rd, Whateley Rd, Newlands Park, Lennard Rd, Croydon Rd, | | |
| Sat | 9.11.40 | Paddling pool at Croydon Rd Recreation Ground | | |
| Sun | 10.11.40 | Wickham Way | | |
| Mon | 11.11.40 | Crystal Palace Park Rd, Oaklands Ave | | |
| Tues | 12.11.40 | Kelsey Park Rd | | 7 killed |
| Tues | 12.11.40 | Manor Way, Whitecroft Way, Hayes Way (Coventry attacked) | | |
| Fri | 15.11.40 | Greenways & Merlin Grove | Pair of parachute mines | 7 killed, 16 injured |
| Fri | 15.11.40 | Overbury Ave, Forest Ridge, Kenwood Drive, Brackley Rd | HEs | |
| Mon | 18.11.40 | Lawn Rd (damaging St Paul's), Beckenham Cricket Club | Pair of parachute mines | |
| Wed | 20.11.40 | Wood Lodge Lane, Sparrows Den, Layhams Rd | | |
| Thurs | 21.11.40 | Foxgrove Rd, The Avenue, Lloyds sports ground Hawes Lane | | |
| Fri | 22/23.11.40 | Oaklands Ave, Woodland Way, grounds of Heartsease, Nash Farm Cottages | | |
| Sat | 23/24.11.40 | Westgate Rd, Foxgrove Rd, Oakwood Ave, Golf Course Beckenham Place Park | | |
| Thurs | 28.11.40 | Rouse farm, Crystal Palace Grounds | | |
| Fri | 29.11.40 | Dykes Way, Mays Hill Rd, Cook's Sports Ground, Romanhurst Ave, Bromley Gardens, Kent House Rd, Durban Rd, Hayne Rd, Beckenham Rd | | |
| Wed | 4.12.40 | Queen Anne Ave | Bomb | 2 wardens killed |
| Sun | 8.12.40 | Kangley Bridge Rd, Kent House Rd, Westmoreland Rd, Woodbastwick Rd, Queensway, Ravenswood Crescent | mostly on waste ground London attacked | |
| Fri | 27.12.40 | Venner Rd, Byne Rd, Forster Rd | | |
| Sun | 29.12.40 | Cator Rd | Pair parachute mines | 1 killed |
| Sun | 29.12.40 | Barrage balloon cable badly damaged on Ibis Field by one of the mines | | possible casualities |
| Sun | 29.12.40 | Lennard Rd, Croydon Rd, Ravensbourne Ave, Foxgrove Rd (great fire raid on city) | Bombs | |
| Sun | 5.1.41 | 13,000 people left Beckenham privately according to food office | | |
| Sun | 5.1.41 | Shells damaged Broomfield Rd, South Eden Park Rd | | |
| Mon | 6.1.41 | South Eden Park area | Bombs | |
| Sat | 11.1.41 | Venner Rd, Cator Rd, Station Rd Penge, Marian Vian School shelter | | |
| Sat | 11.1.41 | West Wickham | Incendiaries | |
| Sun | 12.1.41 | Faversham Rd | AA shell | 1 killed |
| Sun | 12.1.41 | Beckenham baths, Burnhill Rd, Southill Rd | AA shells | |
| Sun | 19.1.41 | St Margaret's Rd, Ancaster Rd, Elmers End, Maberley Rd | 8 bombs | 1 killed, 3 injured |
| Tues | 28.1.41 | Stonepark Ave to Stanhope Grove including Crease Park | 10 small HEs | |

# BECKENHAM BLITZ INCIDENTS AND NUMBERS OF CASUALTIES

| Day | Date | Where | What | Casualties |
|---|---|---|---|---|
| Fri | 31.1.41 | Sylvan Way | | |
| Wed | 5.2.41 | West Wickham | Incendiaries | |
| Sun | 9.3.41 | Well Wood | 8 bombs | |
| Sun | 9.3.41 | Barrage balloon cable in Woodbastwick Rd (London attacked) | | |
| Mon | 10.3.41 | Broomfield Rd, Balmoral Ave, Ravenswood Ave, Langley Rd, Springpark wood | | |
| Sat | 15.3.41 | Wickham Way, Charleville Circus | | |
| Wed | 19.3.41 | 300 bombers on London, Anerley Congregational Church burnt down | Incendiaries | |
| Wed | 19.3.41 | Kingswood Ave, Ravensbourne Ave | HEs | |
| Thurs | 20.3.41 | Cherry Tree Walk, Lime Tree Walk, Queensway, Holland Way, South Hill Rd, Westmoreland Rd, Durham Ave, Kingshall Rd | | |
| Wed | 16.4.41 | Beckenham's worst raid in whole night attack, over 200 incidents using all resources needing outside help<br><br>Beckenham: Lawn Rd, Midland Bank Sports (4), Churchfields/Kimberley Rds, Wickham Way, Ravensbourne Ave(7), Churchfields Rd, Durban Rd (2), Cedars Rd, Foxgrove/Westgate Rd junction, Blandford Rd, Wickham Rd (3), Monks Orchard Rd (2), Links Way, Foxgrove Rd (3), Parkhill Rd (4), Kemerton Rd, Bushey Way, Crystal Palace Park Rd, Bromley Rd, Barnfield Wood Rd (2), Albemarle Rd (5), Shortlands station, Ravensbourne Ave/Ravensmead junction, Croydon Rec, Durham Ave, Court Downs Rd/ Wickham Rd junction, The Avenue Beckenham (4), Barnmead Rd (2), Malmains Rd, Westmoreland Rd, Park Langley golf club (3), Brackley Rd. | | 40 killed including the Stamp household and 3 AFS, 133 injured including Gilbert Crease |
| Wed | 16.4.41 | Border Crescent, Southend Rd, Brackley Rd, Park Rd/Southend Rd, Kelsey Park, Pickhurst Lane | Parachute mines | |
| Wed | 16.4.41 | West Wickham: Cherry Tree Walk, Chestnut Ave (2), Manor Rd, Wickham Chase (2), Grosvenor Rd, Pickhurst Lane, Coney Hill Rd, Birchtree Ave, Queensway, Goodhart Way, Hayes Chase, Hartfield Crescent, Addington Rd, Glebe Rd, Gates Green Rd, Robbins Grove, Staffords Garage, Bourne Way, The Mead (2), Dulverton Rd, Harvest Bank Rd, Pickhurst Rise, Coney Hall Rec, Langley Way, Manor Park Close. | | |
| Sat | 19.4.41 | St Margaret's Villas, Croydon Rd, Wickham Chase | | 11 killed, 15 injured, 150 to rest centre |
| Sat | 10.5.41 | Full moon night, waves of bombers over London, 17 bombs dropped on Beckenham | | |
| Sat | 10.5.41 | Witham Rd, St Margaret's Rd, Sidney Rd, Kendal Rd, Royal Oak Laundry, Elmers End Cemetery, Langley Way, South Eden Park Rd, Pickhurst Rise. | | 11 killed, 15 injured, including 14 year old boy thrown into tree and paralysed |

| Day | Date | Where | What | Casualties |
|-----|------|-------|------|-----------|
| Sat | 10.5.41 | Braemar Gardens between 16 & 18 and Ravenswood Ave according to Peter Tilling and the 1940s house | | |
| Mon | 28.7.41 | Thesiger Rd, Knighton Park Rd | | |
| | 1941 to 1943 | No attacks until Jan 20 1943 but damage from AA shell splinters at Hayes Chase and Sandilands Crescent in 1942 and Abbots Way & Kingsway on 17.1.43 | | |
| | 20.1.1943 | Worsley Bridge Rd, Beckenham Rd near Baths, Elmers End factory workers, Lloyds Bank sports ground, Lawrie Park Rd, Surrey Rd WW | Machine gun and cannon shell fire, two barrage balloons shot up. | |
| | 20.1.43 | Catford school disaster bombed by Fokkerwulf 190; Tony Johns says Messerschmit 109 shot down by Spitfire. No warning. | Planes strafing Beckenham likely to have been from Catford | |
| Wed | 3.3.43 | Sydenham Rd, Ravensmead Rd, Lennard Rd | AA shell damage | |
| | 5.6.43 | Cedars Rd, Durban Rd, Cromwell Rd, Hampden Rd, Croydon Rd, | HE & phosphorus bombs | 1 killed, 6 injured |
| | 5.6.43 | Beckenham named on German radio as target | | |
| Wed | 23.6.43 | Monks Orchard Rd (2) | | |
| | 7.10.43 | Hayes Way, Wickham Way, Elwill Way, Den Rd, Winchester Park, Madison Gns, Celtic Ave, Bromley Gns, Ravensbourne Ave | | 1 killed, 2 injured |
| | 18.10.43 | Sandilands Crescent, South Walk, Westmoreland Drive, Abbotsbury Rd, The Warren, Glebe Way, Barnfieldwood Rd, Goodhart Way | | |
| | 23.2.1944 | 10a Thicket Rd | | 1 killed |
| | 22.3.1944 | The Dell, Hartfield Crescent, WW | | 1 killed |
| | 14.3.1944 | Ash Tree Close | | 1 killed |
| | 3.1.1944 | Clenstone, Tiepigs Lane WW | | 1 killed |

# Fatalities from bombs on Beckenham, including deaths in Beckenham hospital

Fatalities from the bombing of Beckenham WWII, includes deaths in Beckenham hospital

| Date | Place | Dead |
|---|---|---|
| 30.8.1940 | 78 Clockhouse Rd | Mabel Vincent 54, Nellie 40 and Walter 39 Glenny |
| 6/7.9.40 | 101 Bourne Way | Nora Patricia Marfleet 40 |
| | | Vera May Marfleet 36 |
| | | Josephine Sullivan 26 |
| 7.9.40 | 24 Newlands Park | Fanny Elizabeth Irene Scott 64 |
| | | Ethelbert Clark 86 |
| | | Signe Ottilia Collden 63 |
| | | Helen Ann Jones 83 |
| 9/10.9.40 | 102 Oakfield Rd | Nellie Cuthbert Dennison 65 d.18th Beck hosp, after trapped 10hrs |
| | 7 Kelsey Way | William Elswood Ford 52 d.12th Beck hosp |
| 13.9.40 | 6 Southend Rd | Ivy Isobel Clarke 33 |
| | | Doris Louise Mannall 39 |
| | | Marie Isabel Ann Mannall 9 |
| | | Hilda Patricia Mannall 3 |
| | 6A Southend Rd | Mary Isobel Scrivens 36 |
| 14.9.40 to 17.9.40 | 45 Crystal Palace Park Rd | Andrew Douglas Dick 61 |
| | | Elizabeth Dick 60 |
| | 222 Venner Rd | Frederick George William Capron 25 Home Guard |
| | | Joan Eleanor Vince 24 |
| | | Sylvia Joyce Vince 17 |
| | 11 Romanhurst Gns | Samuel George Burton 48 |
| | 19 Crystal Palace Park Rd | Stella Marion Scott Durant 28 |
| | | Alice Clifford 66 |
| | | Egbert Athelstone Carwardine 63 |
| | | Blanche Gwendoline Carwardine 45 |
| | | Frederick Thomas Boyes 49 |
| | | Charles Octavius Aldous 84 |
| | | Nellie Ellum 59 nurse |
| | | Victoria Christian Knowles 53 nurse |
| | | Florence Parker 59 |
| | | Margaret Wilson Mann Sawtell 90 |
| | 65 Kingshall Rd | John Alexander 74 |
| | | Cyril Claude Court 43 Heavy Rescue |
| | | Bridget Court 40 |
| | Courtlands Westmoreland Rd | Lilian Minore Lee 40 |
| | | Elsie Maud Stanford 20 |
| | | Vera Janet Stanford 17 |
| | | Emily Florence Welch 53 |
| | At Capel, West Wickham | Oscar Frederick Evans 47 |
| | | Thomas Evans 76 |
| | New Inn, Hayes | Frederick John Scates 33 d Bromley Hop |
| | | Charles W Hammond 47 |
| 17/18.9.40 | Kenwood Hayes Lane | Emily Elaine Becker 56 |
| | | John Becker 33 |
| | | Philip Becker 31 |
| | | Margaret Bruck |
| 21.9.40 | 61 Kingswood Rd | Sidney Burgess 27 |
| 19/20.9.40 | 138 Victor Rd | George Edmund Dominy 81 |
| | 136 Victor Rd | Frank Charles 70 |
| | | Alice Maud Charles 59 |
| | 2 Tennyson Rd | Frederick Thomas S mith 54 |
| | | James Alfred Smith 19 |

| Date | Place | Dead |
|---|---|---|
| | | May Esther Smith 16 |
| 22/23.9.40 | 72 Belmont Rd | David Guest Hyde 7 |
| | | Ethel Florence Pullar 48 |
| | | Eleanor Jane Smith 37 |
| | 59 Cedars Rd | Emily Clara Drage 69 |
| | | Ada Mary Hughes 60 |
| 27.9.40 | 46 Durham Ave | Arthur Williams 60 |
| | | Alice Williams 59 |
| | Hayes Lane | George Henry Miles 23 |
| | 129 Queen Anne Ave | Katherine Helen Mesher 4 |
| | | Robert Mesher 8 |
| | | Mary Mesher 35 |
| | | Thomas William George Mesher 34 |
| 1/2.10.40 | 8 Links Rd | Percival Boycott Dray 61 |
| | | Elsie Cecilia Lilian Dray 28 |
| | | Eliza Dray 61 |
| 3.10.40 | 200 Croydon Rd | Anthony Arthur Wornell 3 |
| 8/9.10.40 | Elmers End Rd shelter | Florence Emily Willis 62 |
| 9/10.10.40 | 13 Marlow Rd | Bernard John Reardon 26 |
| | | Evelyn Reardon 25 |
| | | Henrietta Maria Reardon 62 |
| 15/16.10.40 | 25 Windemere Rd | Jane Emily Ward 86 |
| | | James Bevis 51 |
| | | Mary Ellen Bevis 50 d Beck hosp |
| 19/20.10.40 | 23 Wickham Rd | Jean Ferguson Robertson 55 d Brck hosp |
| | 30 Den Rd | Walter Henry Goodall 60 |
| | 27 Broomfield Rd | Florence Butler 46 |
| | | Annie Isabel Perman 75 |
| 20/21.10.40 | 2 Birkbeck Rd | Lilian Burgess 54 |
| | | William Edmund Burgess 32 |
| | 4 Birkbeck Rd | William Marsh 59 |
| 23/24.10.40 | 9 Foxgrove Ave | Sidney Gammon 46 |
| | | Frederick David Gammon 18 |
| | | Olive Mary Ulph Gammon 42 |
| 24/25.10.40 | 8A Felmingham Rd | Edward Cooper 9 |
| | | Edward Cyril Cooper 31 |
| | | Ronald Cooper 4 |
| | 27 Bramley Rd | Alice Mary Johnson 79 |
| 28/29.10.40 | Shaftesbury Homes | Dorothy Vera Darrell 15 d Beck hosp |
| | | Ellen Edwards 40 |
| 1/2.11.40 | 2 Belmont Rd | Frederick Chard Howe 64 |
| 2.11.40 | 5A Southend Rd | Mabel Jessie Manly 63 |
| | | Elsie Waller 63 |
| 6.11.40 | Crantock, Bushey Way | Irene Blackmore 38 d Beck hosp, Telephonist ARP report centre |
| 8.11.40 | 169 Venner Rd | James Leonard Houghton 63 |
| 12.11.40 | 15 Kelsey Park Rd | Dorothy Joyce Downer 33 |
| | | Barry Downer 5 |
| | | Keith Downer 7m |
| | | Elizabeth Marpole 70 |
| | | Daisy Elizabeth Grenyer 59 |
| | | Harry John Grenyer 60 |
| | 17 Kelsey Park Rd | Ellen Fox 66 |
| 15.11.40 | 58 Greenways | Cecilia Ethel Sargent 47 |
| | | Leonard Richard Sargent 47 |
| | | John Palmer Sargent 18 |
| | | Brian Richard Sargent 9 |
| | 55 Greenways | Henry Jack Foweather 19 |
| | 103 Merlin Grove | Jessica Redington 43 d Beck hosp |
| | | Mary Anne Florence Drew 76 |

| Date | Place | Dead |
|---|---|---|
| 4.12.40 | 37 Queen Anne Ave | Leslie Frederick Hurst 37 ARP warden |
| | | Gladys Muriel Blinkhorn Hay 48 ARP warden |
| 29.12.40 | St Christopher's Lennard Rd | Hazel Jean Burgess 11 from parachute mine; a second one tangled with balloon cable and came down in the Ibis field on the RAF balloon operators. Casualties not known. |
| 12.1.41 | 25 Faversham Rd | David Albert Putnam 10m |
| 19.1.41 | 11 St Margaret's Rd | Edith June Turner 57 |
| 19.1.41 | 10 St Margaret's Rd | Louisa Georgina Keen 74 |
| 19.3.41 | Anerley Rd | Arthur James Elson 63 ARP controller Penge UDC d Beck hosp 1.5.41 |
| 16/17.4.41 | 92 Blandford Rd | Kathleen Grimes 23 |
| | | Grace Grimes 52 |
| | 94 Blandford Rd | Florence May Popjoy 68 |
| | 76 Churchfields Rd | Jane Fennings 63 |
| | | Florence Edith Keen 35 |
| | 78 Churchfields Rd | George Herbert Benjamin White 35 |
| | | George Cowland 51 |
| | 80 Churchfields Rd | Sarah Anne Watts 57 |
| | | Joseph Tremane Watts 10 |
| | | Virginia Watts 16 |
| | | Albert Edward Watts 61 |
| | | Reginald Tomlin 24 |
| | 151 Churchfields | Charles Greenfield 74 |
| | 133 Albemarle Rd | Clara Wright 70 |
| | 53 Bushey Way | Beryl Winifred Nottage 7 |
| | Church, Shortlands | Hazel Doreen Kissick 18 firewatcher |
| | Church Crescent Rd | Alfred Edward Curtis 59 |
| | Ct Downs/Wickham Rd | Richard Beacon 27 |
| | | David James Chalmers 31 |
| | | Stanley Richard Hudders 30 |
| | Eden Way | Arthur Reginald Trenerry 40 |
| | Midland Bk Sports ground | Maud King 61 |
| | | David Smith 8 |
| | | Ian Smith 5 |
| | | Ivy Winifred Smith 31 |
| | | Raymond Smith 11 |
| | Tantallon | Josiah Charles Stamp 61 |
| | | Olive Jessie Stamp 63 |
| | | Wilfred Carlyle Stamp 36 |
| | | Betty Wark 16 |
| | | Violet Baldock 39 |
| | | Edith Camm 58 |
| | 11 Southend Rd | Lillie Cain 55 |
| | 13 Goodhart Way | Frederick Cyril Griffiths 38 |
| | 200 Wickham Chase | Evelyn Hilda Minshall 28, d 19th Beck hosp |
| | 202 Wickham Chase | Evelyn Margaret Rudham 41 d 12.5.Farnboro hosp |
| 19.4.41 | 11 St Margaret's Villas | Annie Serena Emily Fielder 25 |
| | | Frederick William Fielder 28 d Beck hosp |
| | | William Bert Hall 60 ARP repair services |
| | 13 | Catherine Ann Leach 21 |
| | | Terence Aloysius Leach 13 |
| | 10 | Annie White McKenzie Wickens 19 |
| | 20 St Margaret's Rd | Leslie Arthur Newman 17 |
| | 19 | Daisy Irene Smith 34 d Beck hosp |
| | | Emily Smith 70 |
| | | Bessie Sutherland 26 |

| Date | Place | Dead |
|---|---|---|
| 10.5.41 | 42 Sidney Rd | Rosina Alice Robertson 61 |
| | 44 Sidney Rd | Frank Holton 49 |
| | | Lillian Holton 49 |
| | 22 Kendall Rd | Alice Mary Annie Taylor 64 |
| | 49 Kendall Rd | Helen Mary Tonge 65 |
| | | Mary Helen Whayman 29 |
| | | Mildred Alicia Whayman 58 |
| | 108 Pickhurst Rise | Joan Victoria Linnett 18 |
| | | Victoria Maud Linnett 52 |
| | | William Linnett 56 |
| | 110 | Hilda Beatrice Gosling 41 |
| | | George Henry Gosling 39 |
| | 112 | Frances Mary Nicol 51 |
| | | Frederick Ernest Nicol 41 |
| 28.7.41 | 13 Thesiger Rd | Rose Batstone 61 |
| | | Charles Albert Lowe 24 |
| | | Rosemary Lowe 10m |
| | | Rose Florence Lowe 20 |
| 23.3.43 | Southend Rd | Elsie Amy Hawtin 30 firewoman NFS d Beck hosp |
| 5.6.43 | 43 Cedars Rd | Beryl Dorothy Grover 22 |
| | 64 Durban Rd | Willie Capon 61 d 11th Beck hosp |
| 7.10.43 | 34 Bromley Gardens | Thomas William Munks 49 |
| 7.11.43 | 134 Victor Rd | Jean Hawkes 10 |
| | | John Larry Hawkes 4 |
| | | Kathleen Emily Hawkes 32, husband in RAF |
| | 134 Victor Rd | Harvey Stanley Willcox 64 firewatcher |
| 3.1.44 | Clenstone, Tiepigs Lane | Dorothy Emma Robbins 51 |
| 23.2.44 | 10a Thicket Rd | Hilda Minnie Arnold 45 |
| 14.3.44 | 16 Ash Tree Close | Lydia Seeley 59 |
| | | Janette Nellie Mitton 17m |
| | | Willie John Hardwick 58 Heavy Rescue |
| 22.3.44 | The Dell, Hartfield Crescent | Doris Clouston 20 |
| 25.3.44 | 230 Anerley Rd | William George Melbourne 48 d Beck hosp |
| | 1 Hamilton Place | Mary Jane Sewter 56 d Beck hosp |
| 22.7.42 | Lloyds Bk fire station | Arthur Leslie Tombling NFS d Beck hosp after breaking neck in agility class in diving forward roll |

# The worst night of the war 16/17 April 1941

| Road in Beckenham | Bombs | Names of those killed |
|---|---|---|
| Albemarle Rd | 5 | Clara Wright (70) at 133 |
| Barnfield Wood Rd | 2 | None |
| Barnmead Rd | 2 | None |
| Blandford Rd | 1 | Grace Grimes (52) |
| | | Kathleen Grimes (23) at 92 |
| | | Florence May Popjoy(68) at 94 |
| Brackley Rd | 1 | |
| Bromley Rd | 1 | |
| Bushey Way | 1 | Beryl Winifred Nottage (7) at 53 |
| Cedars Rd | 1 | |
| Churchfields Rd | 2 | Charles Greenfield (74) at 151 |
| | | Mr Cowland (51) at 78, |
| | | Reginald Tomlin (24), |
| | | Albert Edward Watts (61), |
| | | Joseph Tremane Watts (10), |
| | | Sarah Anne Watts (57), |
| | | Virginia Matilda Watts (16) at 80 |
| | | George Herbert Benjamin White (35) at 78 |
| | | Jane Fennings (63),Florence Edith Keen (35) at 76 |
| Court Downs Rd | 1 | Richard Beacon (27), |
| junction Wickham Rd | | David Chalmers (31), |
| | | Stanley Richard Hudders (30), all AFS |
| Crescent Rd | 1 | Alfred Edward Curtis (55) at the church |
| Croydon Rd Recreation Ground | 1 | |
| Crystal Palace Park Rd | 1 | |
| Durban Rd | 2 | |
| Durham Ave | 1 | |
| Eden Way | 1 | Arthur Reginald Trenerry (40) |
| Foxgrove Rd | 3 | |
| Kemerton Rd | 1 | |
| Lawn Rd | 1 | |
| Links Way | 1 | |
| Malmains Rd | 1 | |
| Midland Bank Sports Ground | 4 | Raymond Smith (11), |
| | | Maud King (61), |
| | | David Smith (8), |
| | | Ian Smith (5), |
| | | Ivy Winifred Smith (31) |
| Monks Orchard Rd | 2 | |
| Park Hill Rd | 4 | Violet Baldock (39), |
| | | Maud King (61), |
| | | Sir Josiah Stamp (61), |
| | | Olive Jessie Stamp (63), |
| | | Wilfred Carlyle Stamp (36), |
| | | Betty Wark (16) |
| Park Langley Golf Club | 3 | |
| Ravensbourne Ave | 7 | |
| Shortlands Church St Mary's | 1 | Hazel Doreen Kissick (18) Firewatcher |
| Shortlands station | 1 | |
| Southend Rd | 1 | Lillie Cain (55) at 11 |
| The Avenue | 4 | |
| Westgate Rd | 1 | |
| Westmoreland Rd | 1 | |
| Wickham Rd | 3 | |

| Roads in Penge | Bombs | Names of those killed |
|---|---|---|
| "Ridsdale Rd" | 2 | Ernest Pretoria Tucker (41) at 37 firewatcher and decontamination squad |
| | 1 | Charlotte Llewellyn (57) at 48 |

| Roads in West Wickham | Bombs | Names of those killed |
|---|---|---|
| Addington Rd | 1 | |
| Birchtree Ave | 1 | |
| Bourne Way | 1 | |
| Cherry Tree Walk | 1 | |
| Chestnut Ave | 2 | |
| Coney Hall Recreation Ground | 1 | |
| Coney Hill Rd | 1 | |
| Dulverton Rd | 1 | |
| Gates Green Rd | 1 | |
| Glebe Rd | 1 | |
| Goodhart Way | 1 | Frederick Cyril Griffiths (38) at 13 |
| Grosvenor Rd | 1 | |
| Hartfield Crescent | 1 | |
| Harvest Bank Rd | 1 | |
| Hayes Chase | 1 | |
| Langley Way | 1 | |
| Manor Park Close | 1 | |
| Manor Rd | 1 | |
| Pickhurst Lane | 1 | |
| Pickhurst Rise | 1 | |
| Queensway | 1 | |
| Robbins Grove | 1 | |
| Staffords garage | 1 | |
| The Mead | 2 | |
| Wickham Chase | 2 | Evelyn Hilda Minshall (28) at 200 d Beckenham hospital Evelyn Margaret Rudham (41) at 200 d Farnborough Hospital |

## Types of bombs and weapons

| Projectile | Description |
|---|---|
| Incendiaries | Dropped in large numbers to start fires to mark the target. All businesses had compulsory firewatchers to deal with incendiaries using long handled shovels and stirrup pumps with buckets of water. |
| Sticks of Bombs | Bombs were seldom dropped singly, at least in pairs but commonly in a string across an area. |
| High Explosive | Extremely rapid detonation caused using a booster between the detonator and the burster charge. |
| Unexploded Bombs | Very dangerous as the bomb has a delayed action and were increasingly booby trapped. |
| Phosphorus Bombs | Bombs containing phosphorus burn violently when exposed to air |
| Oil Bombs | Spread black diesel oil over the landing site but did not usually burn. |
| Parachute Bombs (landmines) | The bomb was held back by a parachute and trailing wires so that it exploded on contact and caused widespread lateral damage instead of a crater. |
| Butterfly Bombs | Anti-personnel. Were dropped only once, in Grimsby and had two wings like butterfly wings to entice youngsters to pick them up. |

The **V1** or **doodlebug** was a pilotless mid-wing monoplane over 25 ft long propelled by a pulse engine and carrying an 850kg warhead. It was gyroscopically controlled and carried 180 gallons of petrol which, when exhausted, caused the V1 to fall to the ground. The resulting explosion caused widespread destruction. Almost 9,250 were fired against London but less than 2,500 reached their targets. About 2,000 were destroyed by anti-aircraft fire, 2,000 by fighter planes and nearly 300 by barrage balloons.

The **V2** rocket was the first long range ballistic missile to be used in combat. It hurtled a one ton warhead 50 miles high for hundreds of miles down range to its target and could only be glimpsed as a streak before it exploded.

## The Growth of Rationing in WW2

| | 1939 Sep | 1940 Jan | 1940 Mar | 1940 Jul | 1941 Mar | 1941 Jun | 1941 Nov | 1942 Feb | 1942 Jul |
|---|---|---|---|---|---|---|---|---|---|
| Sweets | | | | | | | | | X |
| Soap | | | | | | | | X | X |
| Milk | | | | | | | X | X | X |
| Clothing | | | | | | X | X | X | X |
| Furnishings | | | | | | X | X | X | X |
| Eggs | | | | | | X | X | X | X |
| Jam & Marmalade | | | | | X | X | X | X | X |
| Treacle & Syrup | | | | | X | X | X | X | X |
| Marge & Lard | | | | X | X | X | X | X | X |
| Tea | | | | X | X | X | X | X | X |
| Meat | | | X | X | X | X | X | X | X |
| Butter | | X | X | X | X | X | X | X | X |
| Sugar | | X | X | X | X | X | X | X | X |
| Bacon & Ham | | X | X | X | X | X | X | X | X |
| Petrol | X | X | X | X | X | X | X | X | X |

**Notes:**

| | |
|---|---|
| December, 1941: | points system was introduced for food, including tinned |
| March, 1942: | basic petrol ration for private cars ceases |
| April, 1942: | illegal to sell 'white' bread |
| June , 1942: | basic petrol ration is replaced by issue of licences |
| 1942 | tea ration for under-fives abolished |
| July 1946 | bread rationed |

Rationing continued after the war and for some items until 1954.

## ID cards and ration book (JL)

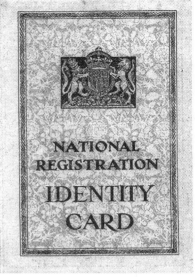

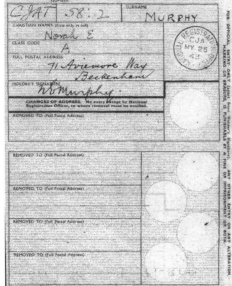

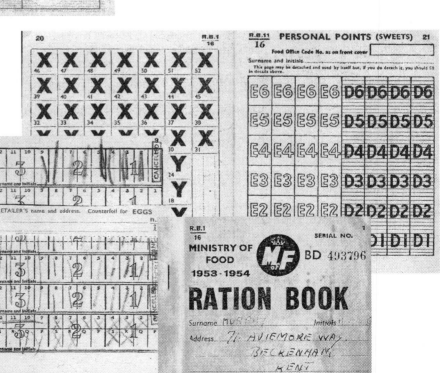

# Time line of major events

## 1935

ARP first formed.

## 1936

**ARP lecture room opened in Old Council Offices, Bromley Road.**

## 1937

**Over 1,000 people attend the Grand Hall of Beckenham baths organised by Cllr Sampson, Chair of the ARP Committee. Great worry about gas attacks.**

## 1938

| | |
|---|---|
| | Gas Masks issued to the public. |
| | Air raid trenches dug in parks. |
| | AFS started. |
| February | Gas mask demonstrations take place in London link. |
| September 15 - 30 | Neville Chamberlain travels three times to Germany to meet Hitler, the last in Munich. |
| | Chamberlain returns with the words: 'peace for our time'. |

## 1939

| | |
|---|---|
| February 25, Saturday | Distribution of Anderson shelters begins. |
| March | Air raid precautions service set up. |
| March 24, Friday | Britain and France guarantee Poland's frontier. |
| April | Conscription begins. |
| August 11, Friday | Trial run for the blackout. |
| August 24, Thursday | Britain calls up military reservists. ARP workers put on alert. |
| August 25, Friday | Britain and Poland sign a Mutual Assistance Treaty. |
| August 30, Wednesday | Warships of Royal Navy proceed to war stations. |
| September 1, Friday | German troops march into Poland. General mobilisation in Britain. Blackout begins. Mass evacuation of schoolchildren, pregnant women and children under 5 with their mothers begins. **London, but not Beckenham, children evacuated. Nonetheless, Beckenham children not allowed in schools without shelters.** |
| September 3, Sunday | 9am the British ultimatum 'that German troops be withdrawn from Poland'. 11am. Britain and France declare war on Germany. 11.20a.m. sees London's first air-raid alert. **Barrage balloons go up over Beckenham and London.** Men aged between 18 and 41 are liable for conscription into army, navy or air force. |
| September 4, Monday | Advance units of British Expeditionary Force (BEF) arrive in France. |
| September 16, Saturday | 'Pool' Petrol introduced. |
| September 22, Friday | Petrol rationed. |
| September 27, Wednesday | Poland surrenders. |
| September 29, Friday | National Registration set up. |
| October | Identity cards issued. |
| October 6, Friday | Hitler offers peace settlement to Britain and France. |
| October 11, Wednesday | BEF strength in France 158,000 troops. |
| October 12, Thursday | Hitler's peace offer rejected. |
| October 14, Saturday | Battleship Royal Oak torpedoed and sunk in Scapa Flow. |
| November 30, Thursday | Following dispute over status of islands in the Baltic, Russia invades Finland. |
| December 3, Sunday | Conscription of all males aged 19-41 introduced in Britain. Females aged 20-30 are required to join women's auxiliary forces or do essential war work |

## 1940

|  |  |
|---|---|
| January 2 | **Beckenham and Penge children from schools West of the Hayes Line evacuated.** |
| January 8, Monday | Food rationing begins. Bacon, ham, sugar and butter rationed. |
| February 11, Sunday | Red Army launches massive offensive against Finland. |
| February 17, Saturday | Further evacuations of British towns and cities link. |
| February 23 | **Churchill's 'Navy is Here' speech commends Captain Philip Vian's rescue of seamen from the Altmark in Norway.** |
| March 11, Monday | Meat rationed. |
| March 29, Friday | Russia declares her neutrality in the European war. |
| April 3, Wednesday | Lord Woolton appointed Minister of Food. |
| April 8, Monday | Germany invades Norway and Denmark. 'Phoney War' nears its end. |
| May 10, Friday | Germany invades Low Countries. Neville Chamberlain resigns. Winston Churchill becomes Prime Minister over a coalition government. |
| May 13, Monday | Germany invades France. Liege falls. |
| May 14, Tuesday | War minister, Anthony Eden, appeals for 'Local Defence Volunteers' LDV. Any piece of countryside on which an invading plane could land is covered with obstacles such as old cars. Pill boxes (small concrete huts for housing machine guns) and tank traps (lines of large concrete 'teeth') are erected in the countryside. **Tank traps in Glebe Way, bricks and wire across Elgood Playing Fields (KPS school). Pill boxes, eg Bridge Road, by railway tracks, disused vehicles in Alexandra Rec.** |
| May 22, Wednesday | Emergency Powers (Defence) Act - defence rules without the consent of Parliament. Previously issued identity cards 'must now be carried at all times'. |
| May 26, Sunday - June 3, Monday | Over 300,000 trapped British and French soldiers are evacuated from Dunkirk beaches. |
| June 4 | **Rescued soldiers on Beckenham Junction to Victoria line trains** Britain in danger of invasion. Churchill's 'we shall fight on the beaches' speech. |
| June 10, Monday | Italy declares war on France and Britain. |
| June 14, Friday | Germans enter Paris. |
| June 18 | Churchill's 'Battle of Britain ..... their finest hour' speech. |
| June 22, Saturday | Armistice between France and Germany. |
| July | Tea, margarine and lard rationed. |
| July 2, Tuesday | Hitler orders invasion of Britain. |
| July 14, Sunday | Churchill refers to the new force of citizen volunteers as the 'Home Guard'. |
| July 19, Friday | Peace terms offered to Britain by Hitler. |
| August 13, Tuesday | Germans begin the systematic destruction of Fighter Command. Battle of Britain has begun. |
| August 15, Thursday | In Battle of Britain, the Royal Air Force shoots down 180 German planes. |
| August 20, Tuesday | In Battle of Britain, the German emphasis shifts to attacking British airports and aircraft factories. Churchill's speech: "Never in the field of human conflict was so much owed by so many to so few." |
| August 26 | **First bombs fall on Beckenham.** |
| August 30 | **First people killed in Beckenham.** |
| September 7, Saturday | Deliberate mass attack on the East End of London starts the intense bombing known as the 'Blitz'. **Beckenham AFS involved.** |
| September 11, Wednesday | Anti-aircraft guns brought into London. |
| September 17, Tuesday | U boat torpedoes and sinks evacuation ship City of Benares. 256 lives including 77 child evacuees. |
| October 30, Wednesday | Neville Chamberlain resigns from the Government due to ill health. |
| November 9, Saturday | Neville Chamberlain dies. |
| December 29, Sunday | The Great Fire Of The City Of London. **Two parachute mines fall on Cator Road.** |

## 1941

| | |
|---|---|
| February | Standard 'National Wheatmeal' loaf introduced. |
| March | Jam, marmalade, treacle and syrup rationed. |
| April 16/17 | **Heaviest raid on Beckenham. 40 killed and 133 injured.** |
| April 21 | **Twenty one Beckenham AFS firemen killed at Old Palace School, Poplar.** |
| May | First consignment of food from U.S.A. under 'Lend-Lease' act. |
| May 5, Monday | Cheese rationed. |
| May 10, Saturday | The last heavy bombing raid of the Blitz on London. 1436 people killed and 1792 seriously wounded. **17 bombs spread over Borough of Beckenham: 11 killed, 15 injured.** |
| June | Eggs rationed. |
| June 1, Sunday | Clothing and furnishings are rationed. link 1 link 2. |
| June 22, Sunday | Germany invades Russia. |
| July | Male conscription extended to those aged 51. |
| July 28 | **Last bombs in Beckenham until January 1943.** |
| August 18, Monday | National Fire Service established, uniting AFS and regular firemen. |
| September | Firewatching made compulsory. Morrison shelters introduced. **Beckenham's Morrison shelters delivered without nuts & bolts.** |
| November | Milk rationed. |
| December 1, Monday | Introduction of points scheme for food. Women aged between 20 and 30 made liable to conscription. |
| December 7, Sunday | Japanese attack U.S naval base at Pearl Harbor, Hawaii. |
| December 8, Monday | USA and Britain declare war on Japan. |
| December 11, Thursday | Germany and Italy declare war on USA. now it is global war. |

## 1942

| | |
|---|---|
| | **No raids on Beckenham this year.** |
| January | American soldiers (called G.I.s from 'Government Issue' words on their equipment) arrive in Britain. |
| February | Soap rationed. |
| March | Basic petrol ration for private cars ceases. |
| April 6, Monday | Illegal to sell 'white' bread. |
| April 21, Tuesday | The BBC broadcasts ITMA (It's That Man Again), starring Tommy Handley. |
| April - June | 'Baedeker' raids on beauty spots like Bath, York and Canterbury. Clothing coupons cut to 48 per year. |
| May 12, Tuesday | First contingent of US Eighth Army Air Force arrives in Britain. |
| May 26, Tuesday | Britain and Russia sign 20-year collaboration treaty in London. |
| June 12, Friday | Basic petrol ration Britain is replaced by issue of licences. |
| June 22, Monday | Defence Regulations introduced to penalise black marketeers. |
| July | Tea ration for under 5s abolished. British civilian casualties for July: 41 killed, 871 injured. |
| July 16, Thursday | Widows' and pensioners' allowances increased by 2/6d per week. |
| July 26, Sunday | Sweets rationed. |
| August 25, Tuesday | Duke of Kent killed in air crash in N. Scotland. |
| September 7, Monday | Up to August last, 597,755 claims made for war damage.have been received. |
| September 9, Wednesday | War Expenditure now running at £12,500,000 per day. |
| September 10, Thursday | British servicemen get 6d (2$\frac{1}{2}$p) a day pay rise. |
| October 11, Sunday | First night-raid on Britain by Luftwaffe for 15 days. |
| October 22, Thursday | British call-up age is reduced to 18. |
| November - December | Allied forces land in North Africa, in 'Operation Torch.' |
| November 1, Sunday | To save raw materials, Government prohibits the manufacture of any furniture except Utility styles. |
| November 4, Wednesday | Afrika Korps defeated by British 8th Army at El Alamein. |
| November 15, Sunday | Production of all private cars in UK banned. |
| December 22, Tuesday | War Graves Commission announce roll of honour for civilians in Westminster Abbey. |
| December 25, Friday | Church bells ring in Britain on Christmas morning as ban is lifted for three hours. |

## 1943

| | |
|---|---|
| January | Utility furniture only available. |
| January 13, Wednesday | Call-up for single girls in Britain lowered to 19. |
| January 20, Wednesday | Daylight raids over SE England by Luftwaffe include bombing of Sandhurst school in Catford, London, killing 44 children and one teacher. **German ME 109 fighter escort planes straffed Beckenham as they fled south.** |
| March 3, Wednesday | 173 die in panic crush at Bethnal Green tube station shelter, due to noise of new AA weapons. |
| April | Luftwaffe attacks on Britain mostly 'hit-and-run.' **Only five attacks on Beckenham from March to November, 1943 with 8 deaths.** |
| April 20, Tuesday | Limited recruitment of women for Home Guard announced. |
| May | Luftwaffe raids on Britain increased. |
| May 13, Thursday | German and Italian troops surrender in North Africa. |
| May 16, Sunday | The 'Dambusters' night attack on the Ruhr; 'bouncing bombs' breach Mohne and Eder Dams. |
| May 20, Thursday | Signposts to be re-erected in rural Britain as fear of invasion fades. |
| June 3, Thursday | First allocation of Algerian wine reaches British shops; 8/- (40p) a bottle. |
| June 5 | **Beckenham named as target on German radio.** |
| June 12, Saturday | King George VI lands in Morocco; his second visit of the war to forces overseas. |
| July | Conscription for women extended to those aged 51. |
| July 10, Saturday | US and British troops land in Sicily. |
| September 3, Friday | Italy surrenders unconditionally. |
| September 6, Monday | Bevin says that demobilization will be much harder than mobilization. |
| September 7, Tuesday | RAF bomb V1 (flying bomb) launch sites on the N. French coast. |
| October 13, Wednesday | Italy declares war on Germany. |
| December 2, Thursday | Ernie Bevin announces conscription to mines as coal output continues to flag. |
| December 16, Thursday | Education Bill: sweeping reforms become the basis of post-war education in Britain. |

## 1944

| | |
|---|---|
| Jan 6, Thursday | In 1943 Bomber Command dropped 157,000 tons of bombs on Germany; Luftwaffe only 2,400 tons on Britain. |
| Jan 20, Thursday | British air force drops 2,300 tons of bombs on Berlin. |
| Jan 21, Friday | Largest Luftwaffe raid on Britain for some time: 90 planes spotted over SE England in 'Little Blitz'. |
| Jan 29, Saturday | Luftwaffe penetrate to London: Davis Cinema, Croydon, receives direct hit but miraculously only seven killed out of 1,250 audience. |
| January - April | Heavy air raids on London and major cities, known as the 'Little Blitz'. **Beckenham largely unaffected with only six attacks with eight deaths.** |
| Feb 17, Thursday | Government publish proposals for comprehensive National Health Service. |
| Feb 18, Friday | Heaviest night raids on London since 1941 as Luftwaffe intensify 'Little Blitz'. Road deaths in Britain for '43: 5,796; more than half occurring during blackout. |
| March 3, Friday | British civilian casualties now total 50,324 dead; military deaths: 50,103. |
| April 4, Tuesday | de Gaulle becomes head of Free French Armed Forces. |
| April 24, Monday | All overseas travel banned in Britain. |
| May - June | Allied forces mass in Southern England for D-day invasion. |
| June 4, Sunday | Allied forces enter Rome. |
| June 6, Tuesday | D-day - Allied forces land on the coast of Normandy, France for the invasion of German-occupied Europe. |
| June 12, Monday | First V-1 rocket attack on Britain. |
| June 16 | **Two V1's fall on Tootswood and Links Road.** |
| August 30, Wednesday | Last V-1 launch sites overrun by British troops. |
| September 3, Sunday | British troops enter Brussels, Belgium. |
| September 8, Friday | First V-2 rocket falls on Britain. |
| September 30, Saturday | Part demobilization of National Fire Service. Those released are liable to military service or to be directed to industry. |
| December 3, Sunday | Home Guard stood down. |

## 1945

| | |
|---|---|
| January 2 | **First of five V2s falls on Beckenham (none in West Wickham or Penge).** |
| January 5 | **V1 fired from Heinkel landed on Lea and Fairfield Roads, damaging Christ Church.** |
| March 27, Tuesday | The last V2 lands in Kent. |
| March 29, Thursday | Last enemy action of any kind on Britain: a 'flying bomb', V1, hits Datchworth, Herts. |
| April 23, Monday | Blackout restrictions lifted. |
| April 25, Wednesday | Allied forces surround Berlin. |
| April 29, Sunday | German forces in Italy surrender. |
| April 30, Monday | Hitler commits suicide. |
| May 1, Tuesday | Britain's remaining ARP workers given one month's notice. |
| May 2, Wednesday | Berlin surrenders to Soviet army. |
| May 7, Monday | Surrender of Germany. |
| May 22, Tuesday | Rations cut in Britain. |
| May 23, Wednesday | Churchill resigns and forms 'caretaker' Government. |
| July 5, Thursday | General election in Britain. |
| July 26, Thursday | Labour gains power with 393 seats. Clement Attlee becomes Prime Minister. |
| August 6, Monday | American forces drop atomic bomb on Hiroshima, Japan. |
| August 9, Thursday | American forces drop atomic bomb on Nagasaki, Japan. |
| August 14, Tuesday | Japan surrenders. |
| August 15, Wednesday | VJ Day (VJ stands for Victory in Japan). |
| September 1, Saturday | Clothing ration reduced by 25 per cent. |
| November 17 | **Harold Macmillan elected MP for Bromley, Beckenham & Penge by-election.** |
| December 20, Thursday | Labour controls end. |

## 1946

| | |
|---|---|
| July | Bread rationed. |

## 1948

| | |
|---|---|
| July | Bread rationing ends. |
| December | Jam rationing ends. |

## 1952

| | |
|---|---|
| February 22, Friday | Identity Cards no longer required. |
| October | Tea rationing ends. |

## 1953

| | |
|---|---|
| February | Sweet rationing ends. |
| March | Egg rationing ends. |
| April | Cream rationing ends. |
| September | Sugar rationing ends. |

## 1954

| | |
|---|---|
| May | Butter, cheese, margarine and cooking fat rationing ends. |
| June | Meat rationing ends. This is the end of rationing. |

## Civil Defence Unit Badges

METROPOLITAN
POLICE
(Inspectors)

METROPOLITAN
POLICE
(Cap Badge, Sergeants
and Constables)

METROPOLITAN
POLICE
(Helmet Badge,
height 4½ inches)

METROPOLITAN
SPECIAL
CONSTABULARY
(Commandant and
Assistant Commandant)

METROPOLITAN
SPECIAL
CONSTABULARY
(Inspectors and
Sub-Inspectors)

METROPOLITAN
SPECIAL
CONSTABULARY
(Sergeants and
Constables)

AUXILIARY
FIRE SERVICE

AIR RAID PRECAUTIONS

CIVIL NURSING
RESERVE

ENTERTAINMENTS
NATIONAL SERVICE
ASSOCIATION

WOMEN'S
VOLUNTARY SERVICES

Women's & Nursing Service Badges

NAVY ARMY & AIR FORCE
INSTITUTES

AUXILIARY
TERRITORIAL SERVICE

WOMEN'S LAND ARMY

THE WOMEN'S LEGION

WOMEN'S
TRANSPORT SERVICE

MECHANISED TRANSPORT
TRAINING CORPS

QUEEN ALEXANDRA'S
ROYAL NAVAL NURSING
SISTERS
(Hat Badge, Gold)

QUEEN
ALEXANDRA'S
IMPERIAL MILITARY
NURSING SERVICE

WAR ORGANISATION OF
BRITISH
RED CROSS SOCIETY &
ORDER OF ST JOHN
(Headquarters Personnel)

BRITISH RED CROSS
SOCIETY

WAR ORGANISATION OF
BRITISH
RED CROSS SOCIETY &
ORDER OF ST JOHN
(For Personnel serving
Overseas)

ST JOHN AMBULANCE
BRIGADE

# Index

# Acknowledgements and Bibliography

Bromley Local Libraries (BL)

Adremians (Beckenham County School Old Girls Association)

Casualties of Kent 1939 - 45 by Imperial War Graves Commission, 1954.

Civilian War Dead, listed by Commonwealth War Graves Commission

Churchill Archives, Chartwell

Churchill Centre website

RAF - Air Historical Branch

BBC - The peoples' war website

Events on the Home Front, website by Peter N. Risbey, 2003.

Flying Bombs and Rockets website, Beckenham Log

Beckenham Journal 1935 - 46 (BJ)

Beckenham & Penge Advertiser 1941

*Badges & Emblems of the Services* by N.A.G. Press Ltd, 1940

*Make Do & Mend* by Board of Trade, 1943

*Wartime Memories* by Doris Pullen, 1989 reprint

*Went the Day Well* by Derek Tangye, 1942; reissued 1995 by Michael Joseph

*St George's Parish Church of Beckenham* by Rachel Notley (RN)

*The Story of Christ Church* by Frank J Clark, 1955 (SCC)

*Bromley in the Front Line* by Lewis Blake, 1983 edition

*London's Hour* (Paintings by Firemen) by Staples Books Ltd., 1942

*The 1940's House* by Juliet Gardiner, Channel 4 Books, 2000

Beccehamian (Boys County School magazines) 1938 to 1940

*Beating of his Wings* by John Hook, London, 1995

*Undaunted* by Graham Reeves, published by Bromley Library, 1990.

*The Day the War Started*, Alexandra Cottages memoirs, compiled by Ms Jo Smith

Log Book of the Girls County School, from Adremian Archives

*Memories of the Many* by Paul Rason, 1995

*Insanity ..... Abounding* by Francis Weiss, Blandford Press c. 1942

*Bombers & Mash - The Domestic Front 1939 - 45* by Raynes Minns, past Times Ed., 2000

*Hitler and my Grandfather* by J W Hilton

*Collected Short Stories & Summer in the Country* by Carey Blyton, Fand Music Press 2002

*Brushes with the Enemy* by Geoffrey Crabb

*Elmers End Congregational Church 1930 to 1941* by Harold Edward Tatman

*Story of the The 101 Surrey Home Guard Rocket Anti-Aircraft Battery, Anerley* 1942 - 44,
by Major W.A. Cooke, December 1944

Family Collection of photos of William Sampson (SC)

London Transport Archives (LTA)

The Extracts from *Summer in the Country* appear by courtesy of the Blyton Estate

The Extracts from *Insanity .... Abounding* are by courtesy of Francis Weiss Junior

Thanks are also due to the Bromley Borough Local History Society, the Copers Cope Area Residents Association, the St George's Church Council and the Home Front Recall project.

We have made every reasonable effort to contact our sources and apologise if we have omitted any from the list above.